JUICE IT
TO LOSE IT

JUICE IT
TO LOSE IT

Lose weight
and feel great
in just 5 days

Joe Cross

HODDER &
STOUGHTON

First published in Great Britain in 2016 by Hodder & Stoughton
An Hachette UK company

I

Copyright © Reboot Holdings Pty Ltd 2016

The right of Joe Cross to be identified as the
Author of the Work has been asserted by him in accordance
with the Copyright, Designs and Patents Act 1988.

A CIP catalogue record for this title is available from the British Library

Trade Paperback ISBN 9781473613492
Ebook ISBN 9781473613508

Typeset in Scala by Palimpsest Book Production Ltd, Falkirk, Stirlingshire
Printed and bound by CPI Group (UK) Ltd, Croydon CRO 4YY

Ho   al,
renew   n in
sustainable   expected
to conf   origin.

In the years since I released Fat, Sick & Nearly Dead, *I've met tens of thousands of people from all walks of life who've felt stuck. They knew they needed to make changes in their lives to improve their health, but just couldn't get over that big hurdle: getting started. To them, I say: 'give me five days.' Five days is doable, it's manageable. It's not 'for ever'. And the way you feel at the end of that five days is so different than the beginning that people tell me it's nothing short of magical or a miracle.*

Thanks to all of you who have had the courage to come to an event, reach out to me on social media, and raise your hand. You remind me why I started this journey in the first place – because everyone needs a little push in the right direction, even if it's from an Australian bloke you've never met.

This book is for you. After all, it's just five days.

Contents

Acknowledgements

Writing a new book is truly a group effort; I'm a great talker, but writing is an entirely different beast. My humble thanks to Jamie Webber, who transformed my thoughts, philosophies and ramblings into a coherent whole, and to Christine Frietchen who smoothed out the rough edges with deft editing. Sarah Mawson was instrumental in forming the thesis of 'Juice It to Lose It,' in addition to coming up with the title.

Warmest thanks to the entire Reboot team: Sophie Carrel, Alison Choate, Kurt Engfehr, Christine Frietchen, Liana Felt, Ameet Maturu, Sarah Mawson, Jamin Mendelsohn, Olaf Steel, Roma Taylor, Alex Tibbetts, Jennifer Vandertoorn, Jamie Webber and Chris Zilo. These folks put their heart and soul into serving the Reboot with Joe community.

Our Reboot nutritionists, Rachel Gargano, Claire Georgiou, Abigail Hueber, Rhaya Jordan, Stacy Kennedy and Isabel Smith patiently coach those on our Guided Reboot Programs, as well as contributing their expertise to our website content.

Thanks as well to the Reboot with Joe Medical Advisory Board, Stacy Kennedy and Carrie Diulus, MD who help me understand the science of nutrition, weight loss and juicing.

Lastly, my thanks to Sarah Hammond and the team at Hodder & Stoughton, and the team at Greenleaf Book Group for their guidance and enthusiasm for Juice It to Lose It.

Juice on!

Chapter 1
Stop Waiting, Start Losing

Have you ever thought about the words 'weight' and 'wait' together? If you put some thought to it, there's some significance there. There are millions of us all over the world who have a goal to lose weight – the problem is we wait for the perfect time to start.

Most of the people I speak to have a fear of getting started. I call it the waiting game. It's a period when you know that you need to make some changes in your life, but you keep putting it off, waiting for the right time. You think 'I'm too busy today, so the diet starts tomorrow,' but then tomorrow turns into the next day, and the next day turns into the next week, and then the next month, and so the cycle continues. Been there, done that.

Reading this book is the first step in the right direction. Follow me, I know the way.

First, a little personal background. I grew up as an Australian kid in the 1970s. It was a time when quick service and fast food restaurants were just starting to spring up. Looking back, it was the beginning of connecting food to 'fun'. I could go and get a burger, fries, a Coke and an ice cream sundae and it was all delivered to me by a man in a clown suit with a red nose. That connection, the one between the food made in these restaurants and my happiness, was made early. I use the word 'food' lightly, because at the time that's what I thought it was. Now I know that it was basically any combination of sugar, fat and salt specifically designed by scientists to hit my bliss point, and boy did my bliss point respond.

It felt like pathways were created between my taste buds and the pleasure centre in my brain that stayed with me through my teenage years. I loved sugar. I wasn't allowed to completely indulge though, because like most teenagers, I lived under Mum and Dad's orders – Our House, Our Rules – which meant limited amounts of soda and ice cream in the house.

When I moved out at the age of 18 and decided to skip college and take a job at the Sydney Futures Exchange, the shackles were off and it became My House, My Rules. Now my refrigerator was filled with red and white: red Coca-Cola cans and white containers of ice cream (usually chocolate).

In my new job as a day trader, I was all about fast cash and a fast life filled with money, expensive hobbies, fancy toys and more food and alcohol than you can imagine. But hey, I was only 18; the human body is an incredible organism that can handle a lifestyle like that when you are young. But it has to end some time.

At 24, I had a little wake-up call after making a fool of myself and blacking out at a birthday party. I knew I needed to change. I'd call this my first attempt at a diet. My goal wasn't to lose weight but I needed a break from the daily cheeseburgers and bottomless wine glasses. I needed to clean up my act. Since I'm an all-in kind of bloke, I jumped head first into an 18-month hiatus from boozing, and I stuck to eating a mostly vegetarian diet. However, around the same time, my professional life boomed. I started my own company and my fast-lane life got even faster. I was rolling in money and that little health stint went out of the window. My body shape started echoing the shape of my wallet. Both were getting fat.

I think I knew deep down that I couldn't just keep hammering my system with late nights, early mornings, and living a life on processed foods. I told myself, 'At some stage, if I keep this up, I will break.' And guess what? I broke. My diet lacked nutrients, I rarely slept, I lived off caffeine and yet I thought I was invincible. But at the age of 32, I developed urticaria, a chronic auto-immune disease that caused a giant rash all over my body whenever I was touched. My body would react to something as simple as a handshake; it was like being bitten by a thousand mosquitoes.

My life changed dramatically. And so began the journey to save myself. It wasn't rocket science; I just went back to basics. I figured that if I'd damaged my health by turning away from Mother Nature and filling my body with junk food, perhaps I could restore my vitality by turning towards her and consuming the foods she intended for us. So I talked to my doctor and decided to consume nothing but the fresh juice of fruits and vegetables. I juiced for 60 days followed by a period of plant-based eating, as you can see in my movie *Fat, Sick & Nearly Dead*. I know that sounds pretty drastic, and it was, but hitting 22½ stone (320 pounds) and suffering from a debilitating disease left me willing to try something radical.

I decided to call my juice fast a Reboot, since my goal was to restart my body and try to regain the perfectly healthy body I had been born with. Choosing to Reboot made me feel back in control. It returned me to the driver's seat of my lifestyle and wellbeing, and it has changed my life for ever.

Before finding the natural healing powers of Mother Nature's fruits and vegetables, I tried all kinds of diets without ever finding a weight-loss solution that stuck. I found a few quick-fix strategies such as going to health spas, eating vegetarian and passing on the alcohol for months at a time, but those periods always came to an end and I went right back to my junk-food and booze-filled lifestyle.

Looking back, I think it's pretty clear why those attempts at regaining my health and a smaller physique didn't work. I wasn't nourishing my body properly. I'd always thought of a diet as a means to remove the foods that weren't good for me, but a Reboot goes much further: it adds in high-nutrient foods so you know what it feels like to truly be healthy and not starved for nourishment. I lost 7 stone (100 pounds) on my 60-day Reboot and 3-month plant-based diet. Today, I still drink juice at least once a day and I'm able to make much better food choices. I have a smaller waistline that doesn't have people asking me when the twins are due. I enjoy exercise. But perhaps most importantly, I'm no longer taking any medications, my mind is clearer, and I'm overall a happier, healthier person.

Thanks to my rollercoaster ride through diet fads and failed weight-loss attempts, I found what worked for me, and it can work for you too. Along with my doctors and nutritionists, I've done the hard work for you. I've figured out what you need to get started. So, if you've been looking for a weight-loss solution that works, you are in the right place. By picking up this book, you've already taken the first step towards getting past the road blocks that are keeping you from weight loss and a healthier life. The second step: love yourself. Loving yourself, appreciating your value, can motivate you to make the decision to change your life. You bought this book for a reason. That's a sign that you truly care about your health. You want to be there for your loved ones, and to wake up every day feeling energized, happy and naturally high on life.

In the following pages, you'll find a simple, foolproof plan to jumpstart a change in your life, your health and your waistline in just five days. I can't wait to see you get started!

Chapter 2
Why It's So Hard to Get Started

O ne of my favourite sayings is, 'Lady Luck follows a person of action.' I used to think that people who were healthy and slim were the lucky ones. But what I didn't think about was that many of them were only like that because they were taking action to control their health and maintain their weight. Some people have their genes to thank, but for the most part, those lucky ones are eating healthily, exercising, managing their stress and getting a good night's sleep. While we can't control the genetic factors we inherit, I've seen first-hand that the more you implement healthy actions, the higher your odds are of becoming a healthier version of the person you are today and maintaining it throughout your life.

The hard part is starting those healthy actions. Jumping into a diet or a weight-loss plan (or any new venture that throws a new pattern in your life) can be a battle all by itself. I've been able to start a handful of weight-loss journeys, but I quickly lost whatever headway I'd made when I backslid into old habits. I wasn't mentally committed, and I wasn't making my health a priority. My 'healthy' periods had a beginning and an end, so the weight always came back. If this start-and-stop pattern sounds familiar, I have news for you. You're not alone. You're not a failure. You're normal.

I've felt this way, and I've met thousands of people around the world who have felt this way too. This feeling can make us feel isolated, helpless and disheartened. We think, 'Why me? Why can't I get my act together and just lose the weight that I've been trying to shed for years?' I've been where you are right now. Over the years I've identified the biggest hurdles to getting started, and how to fix them.

Committing to losing weight and changing the way you're currently living your life may seem overwhelming. Apart from anything else, there are thousands of diet options out there so how are you supposed to know which one works? Keep a diet journal, count points or calories, eat carbs, don't eat carbs, eat fat but not too much, never eat meat, eat meat . . . no wonder many of us don't know where to start or how to do it.

Based on my own Reboot experience, my team of nutritionists and I have created this mini version: a 5-Day Reboot to move past your failure to launch. There's no longer a need to play the waiting game because this plan is straightforward, simple and attainable. It helps you to see past the intimidating early stage of change and understand what it feels like to be properly nourished. So we've done the thinking for you – all you have to do is the juicing. Let's prepare you for lift-off by facing the most common weight loss barriers head-on, and prove that it *is* possible: you *can* lose weight and get healthy and stay that way for the rest of your life.

1. 'Now isn't a good time'

Here's a wake-up call that I learned the hard way: the perfect time to start losing weight doesn't exist. Our lives will always be busy, stressful times aren't going anywhere and we're always going to have plans or a family to care for. When one excuse fails us, we move on to the next. We convince ourselves that right now is just not a good time to start a big lifestyle change. So we wait for that mythical 'perfect time'. But here's something to remember: delaying your start delays the outcome.

I'm telling you that right now is the best time to start. You opened this book because something inside you wants a change – maybe it's the need to lose weight or change your eating habits or naturally manage a health condition (or all of the above). So guess what? Next month is no different to this one. You're ready now and it's time to start. There's no better time!

2. 'I know what I should do, but I just can't do it'

What stops people who want to lose weight from successfully dieting isn't knowing what to do – it's actually doing it. I call it KIVDI. It stands for Knowing It Vs. Doing It. Everyone knows that to lose weight they must eat less junk food, more fruits and vegetables, and move more, yet they go ahead and eat things like pizza, hotdogs and ice cream that are loaded with chemicals and bad fats and too much sodium, all at their own risk. I'm not surprised because I was right there for a long time. The magnitude of change this requires is so great that it seems almost impossible.

It seems crazy that it's so hard. How come we know but we don't do? Something is at work in our brains that leads us to make bad choices. And I reckon it's the processed food that we've become addicted to over the years. It's like a bad drug – it gives you moments of bliss when you fulfil your sweet craving with a chocolate bar, then you feel awful about eating it. But when the next craving comes along, you forget you felt awful and find yourself reaching for that chocolate-chip cookie.

By embarking on this 5-Day Reboot, you're giving your body a definitive break from junk food, and you're going to feel a new kind of addiction, one that is not just good for you, but makes you thrive. The fruit and veggie juices you consume on a Reboot can drastically reduce your bad cravings and you'll find you have new cravings – for natural foods.

3. 'I'm waiting for my "A-Ha" moment'

My eureka moment came to me on my fortieth birthday – I hated looking at the hung-over, fat, sick person staring back at me and I knew I couldn't continue like this or I wouldn't be around for my fiftieth. Sometimes it takes those eye-opening instances to spark something inside our souls to get healthy. If you've already had your eureka moment, well, good on you. Maybe you woke up one day and couldn't button your favourite jeans, or maybe it's come to you in the form of disease or a heart attack or some other life-changing medical condition. This book is a great start because it will put you on the road to optimal health.

If you haven't had a significant wake-up call, stop waiting for one. There may never be a magical moment of readiness. Even that subtle 'I really should lose weight and get healthier' thought at the back of your mind is enough to just hit the Go button. And if you have doubts about whether you can do it, take it one day at a time. The only way to dissolve doubts is through action, and action stimulates motivation. Once you feel the first positive effects of your Reboot, you'll be motivated to continue.

4. 'Thinking about for ever is scary'

Conventional wisdom around losing weight is indeed discouraging. It will not be easy, it will take hard work and commitment to a complete lifestyle revamp – oh, and you have to do it for ever. While it's certainly true that weight loss is a long-term game, feeling like we'll be dieting for ever is discouraging: 'Why bother?' you're probably thinking. 'I can't do this for ever so I won't do it at all.'

So I'm challenging you to not think about for ever – just to start with five days. Think about how fast five days goes. That's totally attainable and will give you a taste of what making a positive improvement could really mean for your health and happiness moving forwards. For five days, you're going to reboot your system. You're going to consume nothing but fresh fruits and vegetables.

After a successful 5-Day Reboot, you will have experienced some initial weight loss and will be feeling great. You will realize that the changes are, in fact, less overwhelming than you feared – and at that point it will be easier to continue and to tackle a longer-term change.

5. 'I'm afraid I'll revert back to my old ways'

Behind the paralysis of not starting a diet lie self-doubt and fear of failure. These doubts will not be dissolved until you take action and actually experience success – until you see that you *can* in fact do it. And guess what? You really can. Negative feelings hinder you from starting something new, and inhibit your visualization of completing it. Stop thinking about what happened in the past; it's OK if your other weight-loss attempts weren't a success. Start thinking about today, because this time it will be different. This 5-Day Reboot is made to give you a fast boost of confidence by flooding your body with energizing nutrients. The faster you feel better, the more inclined you will be to maintain those habits going forward.

At the end of your 5-Day Reboot, you are likely to be a few pounds lighter, you'll feel energized, and – more importantly – you'll feel proud and confident knowing that you can make a commitment to yourself and can successfully follow through. This is the secret to successful change.

6. 'My family and friends aren't supportive of my efforts'

When I first shared my plan to finally get healthy by going on a 60-Day Reboot, some people thought I was out of my mind. I had a few friends who were used to 'Party Joe' and didn't really care about my health. They just didn't want to lose a wingman that would drink beer and eat pizza on any night of the week. But when I talked to my family and close friends, who understood my desperation to get healthy, they were willing to support anything that would help me fight that fight, even though some of them still thought the idea of juicing was crazy.

In my opinion, a strong support network is the key to successfully achieving anything new in your life, especially when you are changing your relationship with food and health. That enthusiasm from friends and family is what sustained me. When it comes to what I call your last two feet of freedom – the distance between the food in front of you and your decision about what to put in your mouth – making the better choice, the choice of a green juice versus a bagel in the morning, is a heck of a lot easier when you are not alone.

We need connectivity in this world. Feeling alone or isolated is a slippery slope that can make us reach out for comfort foods and to self-destruct. Find people in your life who love the path you have decided to take. They might even be inspired to join you. Their support will help you succeed.

If you don't believe that anyone in your close community will support you, then consider a couple of things. First, talk to them. Tell them what you want to do and why. Those hard-hearted people may surprise you and be the most supportive of all. And second, don't be afraid to expand your circle. There are hundreds of thousands of people out there who have either been right where you are or are on this venture with you. That's the beauty of the internet these days. You can easily connect with like-minded people who have either been where you are, or are in the same boat.

Realizing you're not alone – becoming aware there are many, many people going through the same thoughts and feelings – is a life-changing event. Seeing that other people are in our exact same shoes can feel like a huge burden has been lifted. On my website, www.rebootwithjoe.com and on the Fat, Sick & Nearly Dead Facebook page, you'll find a huge community of people who have been in your shoes and are eager to cheer you on.

It's time for action!

Remember my favourite saying: luck follows action. When we feed ourselves more nutrients, we encourage the body we were born with to protect us from harm. But most of all, when we practise skills that improve our life, such as consuming more fruits and vegetables, we start to realize that we can be the CEOs of our own health. It's within your control and with some thought and planning, you'll manage just fine. It is absolutely within your power to change. Just try it for five days.

Chapter 3
A Reboot is More Than a Diet

The 5-Day Experiment

How fun were science experiments when you were a kid? I'm talking about the simple tests that deliver dramatic outcomes. My favourite was adding Mentos to diet soda. If you have ever done this, you will know that a pretty spectacular explosion resembling a geyser takes place. (The carbon dioxide in the soda is attracted to the 40 layers of sugar that coat the Mentos, creating so much pressure that the soda goes flying.)

Obviously you're not reading this book to learn about diet soda and sweets, but you are signing up to have some fun. Yes, that's right. I want you to look at this 5-Day Reboot as a fun science experiment you're carrying out in your adult life. But instead of Mentos and diet soda, you are experimenting with fruit and vegetable juices and your own body. Spoiler alert: the outcome will be an explosion of energy, weight loss and a natural, healthy glow.

Let's keep this experiment simple. Consider every day of your Reboot as a new test – Day 1 is going to be a totally new experience compared to Day 2, and a whole heck of a lot different from Day 5. Each day you'll wake up to new juice recipes, new mindsets and new feelings. You'll be putting your body under the microscope to see what happens when you fill it with the essential nutrients it's been lacking. You'll notice that your body has actually been thirsty for these nutrients all along.

You can think of this book as your science teacher. This is the complete, foolproof guide that will hold your hand throughout every step of this 5-Day Reboot. You're committing to 5 days, not 100, so this experiment is feasible, it's conceivable and I know you can do it. You'll notice that I don't say it will be easy, but when you begin noticing the positive changes in your body, then you'll agree that every headache, bathroom break and irritable mood was worth it. And guess what? Juicing is actually really fun. For many of you, it will be a totally new experience in the kitchen. You can put your pots and pans aside, because the juicer is the only tool you need for this experiment.

Why five days?

Five is the magic number but I didn't pull that number out of thin air. There's a reason I carefully selected 5 as the number of days for your Reboot.

1. Break Through the Atmosphere

On my Reboot and in the thousands of success stories I've heard from others who've followed my path around the world, Day 5 is when the revelation occurs. For years you've been cruising along in that rocket ship called life, encountering bumps and hurdles along the way: aches, pains, illnesses, weight gain and unhappiness. Perhaps you started a diet that sounded like it might work and maybe you got close to breaking through the atmosphere, but the gravity of cravings, negative thoughts and stress kept pulling you down.

With this plan, you're going to soar through the atmosphere but you probably won't feel that moment of calm, non-gravity bliss until Day 4 or 5. The first day will be a new experience because you're getting used to drinking only juice. The next day you might have some detoxification symptoms in the form of headaches, fatigue and fogginess. On Day 3 the symptoms may linger but now you're on a roll, and your skin is starting to look clearer and your energy is increasing. By Day 4 those symptoms are almost gone, but by Day 5, you've hit paradise. Some may even call it ecstasy.

2. Convenience is Key

Even amidst your busy calendar filled with social, work, family and travel commitments, there's probably a period of five days that you can reserve to commit to this Reboot. It's meant to be attainable, not impossible and I reckon anything is possible to do over a five-day period. Not to mention, it keeps the grocery shopping simple. When you go to the grocery store, you're typically buying food for a full week, so we don't want you to have to buy more than that. We've carefully chosen commonly available, inexpensive fruits and veggies to keep your food costs manageable, and each juice recipe has only a few ingredients, so they're quick and simple to prepare in about 5 minutes.

3. Faster Weight Loss, Better Long-Term Results

If you've ever typed 'How to lose weight' into Google, it's likely that most of the advice you'll read says that losing weight at a slower rate is easier to maintain than if the weight is lost more rapidly. But I have some interesting news. According to a study conducted by the Research Department of Human Nutrition at the Royal Veterinary and Agricultural University in Denmark, initial weight loss is positively related to long-term weight maintenance. There is evidence to suggest that a greater initial weight loss as the first step of a weight management programme may result in improved sustained weight maintenance. This is exactly what the 5-Day Reboot is designed to do. It's meant for you to feel the positive benefits as soon as possible because there's no greater motivation to keep going.

4. It's Easy to Take it One Day at a Time

You'll be taking this one day, one juice at a time. That's it. If you've started a diet in the past, the temptation to go all out is common. You're ready to lose weight for good, avoid the junk, start working out and be happier and healthier for the rest of your life. You're ready to commit to for ever and then the diet starts. That sounds all fine and dandy but the problem with thinking about the rest of your life is that it's quite scary. After the first weeks or even days, sticking with every single change starts to feel impossible.

Then the slipping starts.

At first, the slips are minor. You miss a workout due to working late one night and instead of making your healthy dinner you have to order a take-away. Your colleague wants pizza, so you say OK. Soon, those minor slips keep happening and then you're back to square one. But even worse than when you started because now you are depressed that you didn't stick to the diet plan.

That's not going to happen on this Reboot! I want you to look at this 5-Day Reboot with the one-day-at-a-time approach. Wake up each morning and think about how you'll have fun with your juices, how you'll know you're one day closer to feeling better. Be present in each day and practise being mindful. When you bring mindfulness into the equation, especially when it comes to sustaining healthy habits, you'll gain more self-control over your daily choices. You'll gain the power to stay committed to your health. By definition, mindfulness is a state of calm awareness, of paying attention to the present moment with such focus that it's impossible to worry about anything else. So take it one step at a time, and don't worry about tomorrow. Just think about today.

Is Five Days Enough?

At this point you might be feeling a little sceptical: is five days really long enough to make a real change in my life?

My answer? Yes. Five days is enough.

Let's take a visit to your mother's house over the holidays. You spend five days there, and the entire time you are eating all of her classic favourites. A fry-up for breakfast, cauliflower cheese for lunch; supper is buttered mashed potatoes, macaroni cheese and crispy chicken and of course you are having her chocolate cake for dessert – perhaps served with a helping of double cream. And that's just the first day. If you keep that up for five days in a row, you're going to feel pretty lousy when it's time to go home. You'll be bloated, your skin will be drab, you will have gained weight, and you're going to be so tired that all you'll want to do is sleep it off when really you should be working up a sweat.

So if it can take only five days to feel lousy, then I reckon it's safe to say it can take only five days to feel good again. It takes just a day on a Reboot for this process to kick in. In the first 24 hours, certain digestive enzymes stop entering the stomach and instead, other enzymes are released into the intestines and the bloodstream, where they circulate to digest waste and destroy damaged cells without harming the healthy ones.

And the beauty of this plan is that it doesn't have to stop at five days (flip to page 114 for options on what to do next). Some of you may want to stay on this path of just juice because you're feeling so healthy and energized that anything besides juice sounds unappetizing. For others, this is the perfect solution to start eating better. You now know what your body can feel like when it's fuelled with the right nutrition, so you stick to juice for breakfast and maybe go for a snack when the afternoon slump hits. Bottom line, you're re-engineering your taste buds to crave more fruits and vegetables and fewer processed foods, and you have the energy and confidence to make those smarter choices that help your body thrive.

Chapter 4
Reboot 101: How it Works

What's a Reboot?

A Reboot is a period of time where you commit to consuming only fruit and vegetable juices for every meal of the day.

When I first decided to Reboot, I didn't refer to it as such. I considered it a juice cleanse, which it was, but after living through the transformation that juice had over my body, my system was truly rebooted. I was reset, craving more fruits and vegetables and eager to continue on a path of eating healthily. 'Reboot' is the perfect name for it.

By committing to a Reboot, you're getting one step closer to enhancing the quality of your diet. By drinking juice made from fruits and vegetables you're increasing your intake of micronutrients to ultimately improve your lifestyle as a whole and break a cycle of unhealthy eating. When you're flooding your body with this high level of nutrients, it triggers a circuit-breaker that will reset food habits that haven't been benefiting your health.

A Reboot is a straightforward plan. It's not a conventional

diet, so you're not counting calories or counting points or watching your carb intake. You're simply revitalizing your system by consuming 100 per cent plants in the form of fruit and vegetable juices. The nutrition found in these plant foods provides our bodies with the key nutrients we need to help us function optimally. When we're stuck in a rut of consuming too much processed food, we aren't doing our body any favours, and I reckon a Reboot is the best favour you can do for yourself.

Think of it this way. Ten years ago you built a beautiful house. The paint job was fresh, the landscaping was perfect and you were happy to live in such a beautiful home. However, over time you've neglected it. You've never given it a good clean or made any repairs. So what happens? You can't see out of your windows because they are filled with dirt, you have leaks in your ceiling because you never fixed the roof, all of the landscaping has wilted and you're no longer happy to live in your home.

Your body is the same. It's built to feel and look energized, vibrant, happy and healthy. But if you've done nothing but consume processed foods that are lacking in the essential nutrients your body needs, it's not going to work properly. Once damage is done, more damage will occur, which might come in the form of a preventable disease, weight gain, fatigue, etc. A Reboot helps you get back to the way you're supposed to feel. It knocks out all the junk that's been clogging your system. Fruit and vegetable juice works quickly in your body to revive it and truly nourish you from the inside out.

Why Reboot?

Once you get a taste of what it feels like to be well fed and properly nourished, you'll get a big dose of motivation. You're going to want to continue on this path. Some of us can't remember the last time we ate a green vegetable. If we go a long time without consuming the right foods, we start to feel the effects. We feel bloated, tired, experience migraines, our skin breaks out, our middle starts to grow, and eventually this may lead to disease. But guess what? Feeling that way doesn't have to be the norm. A Reboot is designed to remind you of that, to show you that not only can you live a better life, but you can thrive.

So why does a Reboot work if every other diet you've tried has failed?

A Reboot works with your body's natural tendency to reset itself when something's not functioning properly. Because your body has become sluggish from eating too many foods that drag it down, it's often slow to reset itself in the way it would if it were operating at peak capacity. And that's where the Reboot comes in. A Reboot enables you to continue to consume the daily calories you need, filling up on nutrient-dense, sunlight-nourished foods to help restore balance. Once you Reboot, I bet you won't want to go back to those previous destructive habits.

I've met thousands who followed my example after seeing my film, *Fat, Sick & Nearly Dead* and here's what they tell me about their own Reboot: their excess weight poured off, their energy skyrocketed, they decreased their medications and in some cases stopped them all together. They began to think more clearly and their skin naturally glows. Overall they became happier, healthier people. And that right there is how I answer the question, 'Why Reboot?'

Why Juice?

But why just juice? Why not eat the fruits and vegetables instead? Here's how I see it. When you consume only juice, your system is flooded with an abundance of vitamins, minerals and phytonutrients that help your body stay strong and vibrant. Most research shows that diets rich in fruits and vegetables can decrease your risk of certain diseases and I believe one of the easiest ways to get a lot more plant food into your diet – particularly if you're not used to eating it regularly – is to juice it.

How does it work? Juicing removes the insoluble fibre from vegetables and fruits. While fibre is an established, important part of an overall healthy diet, removing the insoluble fibre (while leaving the soluble fibre in the juice) allows for increased absorption of specific health-promoting phytonutrients including enzymes. By removing the insoluble fibre and consuming fruits and vegetables in liquid form, we are providing a nutrient delivery system to our bodies that allows us to consume a much greater quantity of nutrients than if we were eating the whole foods.

Juice is digested rapidly and requires a smaller expenditure of energy than solid food, which gives the body additional time and energy to rid itself of toxins and other unwanted materials that it absorbs. The reason juice works so much better for this purpose is that all the essential ingredients locked within the fibres of fruits and veggies are freed during the juice extraction process, which means those nutrients can be quickly absorbed and used right away by your body.

The idea of juicing might seem a little daunting at first, but that's why I wrote this book – to get you past the doubts and to set you on the right path to losing weight, feeling better and gaining motivation and confidence. Juicing can become a new habit that you'll find quite rewarding. It can help you to supercharge your intake of nutrients without asking your digestive system to work overtime.

I think of drinking fruits and veggies as drinking liquid sunshine – it's like pure gold going right into your system. Most commercial juices that you find on grocery store shelves are processed and lacking in nutrition, while freshly juiced fruits and vegetables are loaded with a richness of vitamins, minerals and phytonutrients.

With every juice you drink you're saying no to processed food. Not only are you making a healthier choice, but you're really putting the highest-grade fuel into your body. You're getting a plant-powered combination of newfound energy, weight loss, clearer skin and a boost to your metabolism.

Juicing + Dinner Option

Up to now, we've talked only about a juice-only Reboot. But we've also included a variation: juicing all day except for a plant-based dinner.

Adding a dinner option to this plan provides two main benefits: the convenience of eating with your family, and the ability to accommodate social or work events. While sticking to all-juice is likely to result in a bit more weight loss during the five days, for some people having the option of a healthy dinner can make sticking to the plan a bit easier. For those with families, it eliminates the need to make two different dinners, which often happens on other weight-loss plans.

So which is better: juice only or juice + dinner? I like to think of it like this. We're all in a swimming pool together. Some of us might have waded in slowly, some have jumped in from the side with a cannonball and others have plunged into the water after doing a backflip off the diving board. But whichever way we've gone in, we're all equally wet. We got in the pool based on what worked for our individual comfort zones, and we're all swimming now.

And you'll still be swimming in a sea of fruits and vegetables even if you choose a dinner option. This doesn't mean you get a free-for-all, but you can sit down with your family at the end of a long day and put your own fork and knife to good use.

1. Eating with Your Family

Many of you are probably the cook in your household. If it weren't for you, your family would starve! Well, not really, but thanks to you, food is on the table. When you're doing a juice-only Reboot, it can be quite challenging to cook for others. You're at the head of the table sipping on juice while everyone else is eating what you just worked hard to prepare. With the dinner option in this 5-Day plan, you're able to enjoy the best of both worlds. It allows you to start incorporating healthier meals for your family, while also staying committed to your Reboot plan. Think about a rich and spicy chilli, colourful salads, or a delicious stir-fry. Our dinner options are designed to be delicious so your family will enjoy the new recipes too. They are also simple to make so you aren't spending hours in the kitchen.

2. Attending Work or Social Functions

If you're busy with work functions or can't miss your best friend's birthday dinner on the week of your Reboot, you can still be social. While this may not allow you to get home to your kitchen and cook your own meal, you can use our dinner options to inspire you to choose what to order from a restaurant menu. I typically go for a salad loaded with veggies and fruit only. Remember, a Reboot doesn't include nuts, beans or seeds either, so stick to the fruits and veggies. Take a look at the sides they offer. Side dishes of sautéed spinach, kale or roasted sweet potatoes are some of my favourite options. And don't hesitate to ask the waiter if they have any vegetable-only entrée options. You might be surprised as to what they can come up with. Avoid the alcohol too. Just because wine is made from grapes does not mean it is part of a Reboot plan!

As for me, I didn't include the dinner option during my own 60-day Reboot. I knew that if I allowed myself to start chewing, it might trigger my old junk-food cravings and I might end up with a pint of chocolate ice cream in my hands. I don't love admitting that, but I'm only human and I will admit, sugar is one of my weaknesses. So, I find it easiest to stick to juice only. Sure, I go to a lot of dinners when I'm Rebooting, but I find it makes the conversations more interesting with a juice in hand. Everyone starts to ask, 'What's that you're drinking?' You never know who you might inspire to start their own health journey when you're drinking your juice in public places.

REBOOT RECAP

A Reboot is a period of time when you commit to consuming only fruit and vegetable juices for every meal of the day. By drinking juice made from fruits and vegetables you're increasing your intake of micronutrients to give your body the nutrition it needs, while breaking the cycle of unhealthy habits. A Reboot is a time for the body and mind to reset and maximally absorb micronutrients and phytonutrients to allow for a transition to healthier, wholefood, plant-rich eating behaviours. Don't think of it as taking something away from your daily diet but, rather, adding in high quality sources of nutrients.

A Reboot, followed by a healthy lifestyle helps you:

- Boost the number of fruits and vegetables you consume daily

- Break the cycle of unhealthy eating and crave healthy foods

- Jumpstart a weight-loss plan

- Manage a healthy weight

- Increase energy levels

- Promote healthy skin, nails and hair

- Ease digestion by accessing digestive enzymes locked away in whole produce

Chapter 5
What to Know Before You Begin

As with any new endeavour, planning is key because the more prepared you are, both physically and mentally, the more ready you'll be to launch into your Reboot successfully. Guess what? I was not prepared! I didn't have a juicer. I also ate more junk than you can imagine the night before I started (a burger and French fries were only the half of it). Looking back, it's a miracle I made it through the first day. So let me spare you from making the same mistakes I did by sharing everything you need to know to fully embrace this plan and make you feel at ease as you gear up for your five-day juicing journey.

You Need a Juicer

For some of you, this may be stating the obvious. But as I mentioned, I didn't have one. I had the camera crew ready to start filming me on this new journey, and that was about it. Don't do what I did and run out to the store the night before to purchase your juicer. Get that taken care of now, so you can get it set up on your kitchen counter and maybe even start experimenting with it early. (For help selecting your juicer, see Choose Your Juicer on page 50.)

A Juicer is Not a Blender

This confusion is one of the most common misunderstandings I've come across since sharing my juicing journey. Both are great ways to include the rainbow of produce in your diet, and also to consume a greater variety than you may otherwise eat. But blending and juicing are different and it is important to understand why.

> **The Two Main Types of Fibre**
>
> **Insoluble fibre** (which is expelled in the pulp) helps to keep the bowels regular and adds bulk to your stool. Insoluble fibre fills you up and speeds up the passage of food through the digestive tract.
>
> **Soluble fibre** (in juice) absorbs water like a sponge and provides bulking matter that acts as a prebiotic to support good bacterial growth and digestive health. It also helps regulate blood sugar and may lower blood cholesterol. Soluble fibre slows the transit of food through the digestive tract and helps you feel satiated.

Blending: When you make a smoothie, you are adding whole fruits and vegetables into the blender. You turn the blender on and it pulverizes the whole produce. Nothing is being extracted; everything – the insoluble fibres and soluble fibres – remains in your smoothie and is consumed when you drink it.

Juicing: When juicing, you are adding whole fruits and vegetables into the juicer but this machine extracts the liquid and most of the nutrients the produce contains. This liquid I'm referring to is your juice. The juicing process removes the insoluble fibre – the pulp – which is deposited in the juicer's collection basket.

Don't get me wrong. Fibre is good for you. It keeps your digestive tract healthy and it slows down the absorption of sugar. But it also slows down the absorption of nutrients and some nutrients stay in the fibre, passing through the body unused. When you juice, you are extracting up to 70 per cent of the nutrients right into your glass, and without the insoluble fibre your body may be able to more easily absorb those nutrients.

So there's a very clear distinction here and you can simply ask yourself the question, is the machine removing the pulp? If not, it's not juicing.

When you're Rebooting, you're juicing. After your Reboot, blended smoothies are a great addition to your diet, but for these five days, we're all about juicing.

Bottled Juice vs. Fresh Juice

Many people wonder if they can drink bottled juices on a Reboot and the answer might surprise you because, yes you can. You just need to take some care in choosing between brands and types of bottled juice. Unlike fresh juice, bottled juices must be treated to kill any bacteria and extend the shelf life of the product. A newer bottling and sterilization process called High Pressure Processing (HPP) makes drinking certain bottled juices a great choice when you can't find fresh. This type of process subjects the juice to very high pressure, which kills bacteria but not the beneficial enzymes and phytonutrients. You can, therefore, drink some bottled juice on a Reboot. When shopping, look for the terms 'HPP', 'high-pressure pasteurized', 'high-pressure processed', 'cold-pressed', or 'cold pasteurized' on the label.

HPP allows the juice to be stored for longer periods of time and happily consumed knowing you are still receiving much of the nutritional content that the fresh juice has to offer. It's not a matter of which one is better but the bottom line is, I'm a huge fan of fresh juice. Making your own or going to your local juice bar for a fresh one is, in my opinion, the best option. But drinking a juice is better than no juice at all, which is why HPP juice is the next best thing.

If you do choose to incorporate bottled juice, check the labels carefully. You're looking for a ratio of around 80 per cent vegetables to 20 per cent fruit. Many commercial juices include a much higher amount of fruit, making them too high in sugar and not high enough in micronutrients for the purposes of your Reboot.

The Importance of Getting Enough Liquids

This probably comes as no surprise, but staying hydrated during your Reboot might be one of the most important factors in making it a success. Water is vital for nearly every metabolic function in the human body. When I did my Reboot, I experienced some dizziness, headaches and fatigue because I wasn't drinking enough water in addition to juice. Our Reboot nutritionists highly recommend consuming additional water during the Reboot to help you lessen or avoid those issues.

Why do we need the extra fluids? When we are ingesting so many nutrients our pathways of detoxification re-adjust themselves, allowing for the increased excretion of metabolic waste. We need that extra fluid to assist in these processes to ensure the adequate disposal of these wastes through our urine and bowel movements (and of course sweat if we're exercising).

On the 5-Day Reboot Plan, in addition to the requirement of drinking 1.5–2 litres/48–64 ounces of filtered water per day, we recommend drinking warm lemon water in the mornings and coconut water or vegetable broth as a snack. Here's a quick look as to why these specific liquids are part of the plan:

Lemon Water

Warm lemon water aids the digestive system and eases the process of eliminating waste products from the body. It prevents the problems of constipation and diarrhoea that can be experienced on a Reboot.

Lemon water is especially important on a Reboot because it's rich in vitamin C, which helps to boost the immune system; it also contains anti-inflammatory properties, has anti-aging benefits and offers a natural energy boost. Drinking lemon water is one of those healthy regimens that you'll probably find yourself addicted to even beyond your Reboot.

Coconut Water

I didn't drink coconut water during my Reboot but I wish I had. I think it really would have helped alleviate many of the symptoms I experienced in the first few days, including light-headedness, dizziness, fatigue, headaches and brain fog.

Coconut water provides a healthy source of electrolytes. Electrolytes pretty much do as they sound: they electrify your system. They are ions that carry electricity through your body. Common electrolytes include sodium, chloride, potassium and magnesium, and are essential for the normal functioning of our cells and organs. You lose electrolytes when you sweat, and you replace them by drinking fluids.

If you don't like the taste of coconut water, try adding a squeeze of lemon. Or try mixing half of your favourite juice with half coconut water. That will help reduce the coconut flavour and might even help you acquire a taste for this tropical treat. As for me, I like adding lots of ice so it's super cold. It just tastes better to me that way. If coconut water really isn't your thing, or you cannot find it in your grocery store, you can drink vegetable broth as an alternative (more on that below).

Vegetable Broth

I like to Reboot with the change of seasons. I figure since Mother Nature is reviving her system, then so should I. So when autumn and winter hit, I'm yearning for something a little warmer than juice. Including vegetable broth as an option on this 5-Day Reboot offers you warmth and a high dose of nutrients, not to mention being a perfect way to use your leftover juice pulp! You can find our recipe in the Extras (see page 127). I also like including vegetable broth just for variety with a more savoury flavour since the majority of the juices you will be drinking are on the sweeter side.

Keeping Costs Down

'Buying fruits and vegetables is too expensive!' I understand why it's a concern, and that is why we have specifically designed this 5-Day plan to keep your juicing costs down. Here's how:

Common, High-Yield Fruits and Vegetables

You won't find anything exotic on this plan. We're sticking to the basics. Each juice recipe is made up of common produce that's typically on grocery store shelves all year long. Produce has also been carefully selected to result in a high yield, meaning every fruit or vegetable you add to your juicer will produce a hefty amount of juice. The 5-Day plan includes common favourites like cucumbers, celery, apples, oranges and pears.

Use Any Greens

Of course, greens are a main ingredient in many of our juice recipes in this plan. Green leafy vegetables win the gold medal when it comes to nutrition. They are high in vitamins, minerals and phytonutrients such as vitamins A, B, C, E and K, iron, magnesium, manganese, calcium, folic acid, carotenoids, omega-3 fatty acids and chlorophyll. Greens support a healthy immune system, help reduce the risk of cancer, support a healthy metabolism, aid in weight control and reduce cravings – the list goes on. And for anyone concerned with protein intake, juices high in dark leafy greens have the most protein per serving.

We know that finding certain greens might be a challenge depending on seasonality and where you live, so in our recipes, although you will see a recommended green that we think is best in the recipe, you are welcome to use any greens. You can choose between kale, chard, romaine lettuce, spinach and spring greens, depending on what's available at your market, what looks the freshest and what's at a good price.

To get the most nutritional benefit, it's important to

vary your greens throughout the five days, so try to mix it up.

Organic vs. Conventional Produce

When I Reboot, I try to purchase organic produce, but if you're stressing about the price, stop right there. To me, the benefits of a diet rich in fruits and vegetables outweigh the risks of pesticide exposure. Remember to wash all your produce well. When conventional produce has a peel, remove it. If you have a local farmers' market, take advantage of what they have to offer. They may not technically be listed as organic, but they're a better choice than selecting imported produce that's been sitting on a truck for days.

What is organic anyway? The term 'organic' refers to the way farmers grow and process their products. Instead of using chemical weed killers, herbicides, insecticides, antibiotics and hormones, organic farmers use natural fertilizers, beneficial insects and birds, and crop rotation. If you're worried about organic produce putting a hefty dent in your wallet, the Environmental Working Group (EWG, www.ewg.org) has broken down which fruits and vegetables are likely to have the most pesticides, and those are the ones you should buy organic when possible. They call it the 'Dirty Dozen'. The good news is that there's also a 'Clean Fifteen', so if you're concerned about the price, you can select conventionally produced fruit and vegetables from that list.

Among common juicing ingredients, these conventionally grown ingredients are most likely to have a heavy pesticide residue. Try to buy the following organically, if possible.

- Apples
- Celery
- Spinach
- Sweet red or yellow (bell) peppers (capsicums)
- Greens

These conventionally grown items tend to have the least pesticide residue, so pesticide exposure should be lower:

- Pineapple
- Sweet potatoes
- Cabbage
- Grapefruit

Source: Environmental Working Group 2015 'Dirty Dozen' and 'Clean Fifteen'

Five Ingredients or Less

Simplicity is the goal for this 5-Day plan, so you won't see any juice recipes that are complicated, require lots of chopping and peeling, or take too much time. Most juice recipes contain five ingredients or less. Don't worry, we aren't sacrificing the flavour here, we've hand-selected each juice to appeal to all taste buds. Here's the thing about juicing: you may find that you can't stand eating cucumbers, but you love them in a juice. Don't be hesitant to step out of your comfort zone. You'll surprise yourself at how you may come around to celery after all.

Cooking for the Family

When you're cooking for your family the thought of drinking only juice can seem like an overwhelming, almost impossible task. 'How am I supposed to whip up mashed potatoes without eating any?' you say to yourself. Over the years, we've gathered the best tips from our Reboot community who have made it work. Their tips are practical, simple and quick, and will put your worries at the wayside.

1. **Make your juice first,** then prepare dinner for the rest of the family. Then, as you're cooking, you can sip on your delicious juice to help satiate your hunger/ temptation. You can even pour your juice over ice into a fancy wine glass so it feels like a special treat.
2. **Use a juice recipe in the plan to inspire you to make a salad** for your loved ones. This helps the shopping process because you will be purchasing the same foods, just in larger quantities. If a protein food such as wild fish or grass-fed meat is on the family menu, pop it in the oven while you're assembling the salad.

3. **Include your family in the process.** Kids love juicing. It's like a fun game for them. Encourage them to come up with your next juice recipe, help you shop for the best produce, and add the ingredients through the juicer. Let them invent a name for your juices.

4. **Share your juice!** Your spouse or partner may not want to Reboot, but that doesn't mean they can't enjoy juice. Sharing is caring, and in this case I mean that literally. You're literally showing you care for your loved ones' health by letting them enjoy some of your juice.

5. **Create family goals that go beyond your Reboot** such as 'Once a week we'll all try a new vegetable' or 'Twice a week we'll all go to the park together and run around and play for at least 30 minutes.' Give everyone something to be working on. When your family is on board, a healthy lifestyle is more achievable beyond this 5-Day Reboot.

6. **Find support.** It's so much easier to do something when you surround yourself with others who agree with your goals and will help encourage you. If you can't find that in your immediate family, you may want to spend a few hours of your 5-Day Reboot with a good friend who will.

7. **Don't be afraid to step away.** If you're feeling particularly vulnerable one evening, separate yourself from the family meal. Go and catch up on a film in the bedroom with your juice while the family eats. You're allowed to put the focus on yourself for once.

Juicing with Health Conditions

The reason I started juicing was so that I could alleviate the symptoms of the auto-immune disease I had, which caused me to break out in hives at the touch of a hand. For me, my 7-stone (100-pound) weight loss was a bonus. Was it a health condition that led you to buy this book? Good on you, because with the help of your doctor, I believe that even just five days can begin to transform your health and help you feel better. For those specifically with diabetes and thyroid conditions, there are a few things you should know because your plan might need to be adjusted to suit your specific health requirements.

Diabetes

There are many people who suffer from the detrimental effects of diabetes, but here's the encouraging news. Many people with diabetes have successfully participated in both juice-only and juice-plus-food Reboots, jump-starting into a healthy lifestyle and even decreasing and sometimes eliminating the need for medications.

But if you have diabetes it's important to customize your Reboot plan, taking certain factors into consideration. First, always consult with your doctor before starting a Reboot. For anyone taking insulin or other diabetes medications, it is especially important to discuss how to adjust your medication appropriately during your Reboot. (For more information see Talking To Your Doctor, on page 166.)

If you have diabetes, we recommend modifying your Reboot as follows:

- Consider the dinner option. The extra fibre from whole vegetables and fruits will help keep your blood sugar steady.
- Pay extra attention to hydration and drink plenty of water. When you're dehydrated, your blood is more concentrated and sugar levels can be higher.
- Stay active – exercise has its own way of helping keep blood sugar levels in check. While strength training is important, regular cardiovascular exercise has been shown to have the greatest positive impact on diabetics.
- Talk to your doctor, who may suggest decreasing the amount of fruit in some juices, or choosing mainly vegetable juices.

Thyroid Conditions

A concern for anyone with a thyroid issue is that eating raw cruciferous vegetables (officially called brassicas) might further suppress your thyroid hormone function and may also interfere with your body's ability to lose weight. So, if you have a thyroid issue, pay close attention to your veggies. Avoid consuming large amounts of raw cruciferous vegetables including broccoli, cauliflower, Brussels sprouts, bok choy, cabbage, kale, radishes, mustard greens and collard greens. For the 'any greens' option in the juice recipes, your best bet is to select romaine lettuces, chard or spinach. We've included substitution suggestions for cruciferous vegetables in our recipes.

Cruciferous vegetables are certainly healthy and have been shown to support the liver in its natural detoxification processes, so if you select the dinner option, you can enjoy these vegetables cooked.

What to Expect from Your Body

I find it pretty remarkable how much the body can transform itself in five days. But before you get to that breakthrough point, there's no denying that the first few days are going to be a big wake-up call – especially if you do what I did and go out and binge on burgers, fries and milkshakes the night before. Sadly, that wasn't the only time I did that. That was how I ate regularly. The more processed food you eat on a daily basis prior to starting your Reboot, the more challenging you'll find the first few days. There's a reason we recommend a soft 'transition in' period, which you can learn more about on page 58.

One of the toughest ideas to accept is that you won't be chewing food for five days, unless you choose the dinner option. Even then you're still going an entire day without putting those pearly whites to good use. That's pretty tough when we live in a world where our social, family and work lives revolve around our next meal. Beyond mentally missing the act of chewing you might find yourself hungry. If this happens, make another juice or drink another glass of water.

And be aware: feelings of hunger are often food cravings in disguise. You might experience a few symptoms in the first three days such as headaches, fatigue, light-headedness, constipation or diarrhoea, increased body odour or bad breath. Your first few days may not be easy, but remember – it's only a few days.

Don't let these challenges scare you. I promise you, I'm not a bully who gets joy out of seeing you suffer. The harsh truth is that the more misery you feel in the first few days, the more you probably needed this Reboot in the first place. There's a reason you're not feeling good. Your body is in overdrive, dealing with all the junk you've put into it, and you are beginning to break certain eating habits you've had for a lifetime. Feeling overtired, anxious and headachy is normal, but know that you won't feel this way for much longer. You'll get through it. Soon you will break through the atmosphere and the rocky start will turn into a feeling of bliss. You'll be floating in a world without anything weighing you down. How good does that sound?

Chapter 6
Prepare to Launch Your Reboot

Set Up Your Environment for Success: Discard the Temptations

When you think about how you're going to be successful on this 5-Day Reboot, I want you to consider two scenarios:

Scenario 1: You've decided to fill a decorative bowl in your living room with mouth-watering chocolates. You think it makes your home more welcoming, and a little sweeter for guests. It starts to become a habit to take a stroll past the bowl every day and enjoy a few bits and pieces. Then your child opens the bag of crisps that you've been trying to avoid. Now that they're open, why not have a few handfuls? When you go to make tea at the end of the evening, you notice that a jar of peanut butter is sitting right next to all of the teabags waiting for a little spooning action – the kind that involves you scooping a huge serving right into your mouth.

Scenario 2: Your decorative bowl is filled with a potpourri of your favourite scent. Your child comes home and looks for crisps, but you haven't bought any so he opens the bag of baby carrots and leaves them on the counter. When you go to make your tea at the end of the evening, the only thing next to the teabags is more tea.

Scenario 1 tests your willpower. Sure, willpower matters, but that can't be the only strategy you're depending on to keep you on track. I know that for me, when I started my Reboot, my willpower wasn't strong enough to withstand my temptations, so I stayed away from my weak spots.

By its very nature, willpower comes and goes. And when you need it most, it's hard to find. So instead of using your willpower to help you stay on course during your Reboot, let's take it out of the equation completely. A different technique to consider is to 'pre-commit' to your Reboot. Pre-commit by literally scrubbing your environment of temptations so that testing your willpower won't be a worry for this part of the journey. If you're constantly surrounded by temptations, the more you face them, the weaker you become and eventually you're eating the chocolate, the crisps and the peanut butter.

Brian Wansink, Director of the Food and Brand Lab at Cornell University, is an expert on how our environment induces us to overeat. In my second movie, *Fat, Sick & Nearly Dead 2*, we visited a bakery where he showed me how a grocery store can wear down your resistance to buying a snack by the way the items are presented. It was an eye-opener to say the least, and led me to understand an important truth: that much of the junk that we snack on is determined not by what our bodies are telling us, but by 'triggers' on the outside.

This sort of basic 'change your environment' approach is all the more important when we realize that urges to eat while you are juicing may seem impossible to ignore at the time, but if you just give it a few minutes, that sudden desire will pass. A lot of what people call 'willpower' is just a matter of staying out of harm's way until your hankering passes.

So here are some simple but effective suggestions to make your environment ready for your Reboot.

1. **Don't Stock Your Temptations.** This seems obvious but it's really important. If you don't keep biscuits in the cupboard, your chance of eating them goes way down, because now you'll have to get in your car and go and buy them. It's just too easy when they're sitting there at home, calling your name.

2. **Play the Delay Game.** One big characteristic of those who maintain healthy diets is their ability to delay gratification. If the sudden urge to eat hits you while on your Reboot, give it a minute. Make another juice, take a walk or call a friend. I guarantee, in less than 30 minutes you'll forget you ever wanted to dive into those unhealthy desires.

3. **Avoid Your Weak Spots.** We all have weak spots. For me, it's the chocolate bowl. If that was in front of me,

it would not last long. It's OK to admit that we just need to avoid our temptations altogether. Maybe for you, it's hard to drive past your favourite ice cream shop on your way home from work. So make it easier on yourself by taking another route home, or have a juice with you for the drive so you're enjoying something sweet.

4. **Discard the Junk.** I'm not a fan of waste, but if it comes to setting up your environment to help you successfully Reboot and lose weight, then there are steps you can take to get the junk food out of your house. Clear out all the processed foods and snacks you find tempting, put them in a box and take them to your local homeless shelter or food bank.

5. **Remind Yourself, You're Worth It.** Believe in yourself. Deep down, truly believe that making all of these changes is worth it, because you're worth it. You were only given one body and one life to live on this planet so it's up to you to make the best of it. Almost all of us are harsher on ourselves than we would ever be on a loved one, but nothing good can come from constantly beating ourselves up. No one is perfect and it is completely normal to experience a bump in the road. We can't control our past, so it's important to forgive and move forward. Do something as simple as putting Post-it notes on your mirror every morning reminding you how special your life is and how important your body is.

With each day of your Reboot, and each day that you're enjoying more fruits and vegetables in your diet, your palate, senses and appetites will start re-engineering away from nutrient-void, processed foods, and begin to crave fruits and vegetables. This makes it easier to break the junk-food cycle than trying to do it through sheer willpower. Believe me, because I tried white-knuckling it and all it did was drive me back into the comforting arms of my bowl of chocolate ice cream.

Setting Up the Kitchen for Success: Juicing Tips

Now that your environment is set up for weight loss success, let's get it set up for JUICING success. I'm sharing the best tips I've gathered personally and from others over the years.

Choose Your Juicer

First and foremost, you need to buy (or borrow) a juicer. Whoever said you can't buy your friends has never had a juicer because I reckon the juicer is like your best friend throughout the Reboot. It's the tool that generates the nutrients you need for your five days of juicing. But this friend won't leave you after five days – you'll want this to be a bond you'll have for ever. So if the initial price-sticker shock scares you (good juicers start at about £100), remind yourself this is something you are investing in for your long-term health.

Remember – you don't have to buy now! Juicers are one

of those appliances that people tend to receive as gifts, or they buy a juicer with healthy intentions, but today that juicer is collecting dust. Check Craigslist, eBay, or simply ask your friends – chances are, someone will lend you their juicer if you're not ready to buy one.

Here's what to consider when choosing a juicer:

The size of the feeder tube

Cut your juicing time down by selecting a juicer with a wide feeder tube (7.5 cm/3 inches is ideal) so most whole fruits and vegetables easily fit.

Ease of cleaning

The ugly truth about juicers is that they are not easy to clean, but some are definitely easier to clean than others. Look for a juicer that has dishwasher-safe parts so your clean-up can be simple and fast.

The pulp-ejection system

Some juicers collect the pulp in an internal basket while others eject the pulp into a bowl or a pulp collector that is specifically sized for the juicer. We recommend buying a juicer that ejects the pulp externally, since this allows you to make larger quantities of juice without having to take extra time to stop your juicer, open it up, and empty the basket.

Multiple speeds

Having multiple (at least two) speeds allows you to extract the most juice out of your produce. Slow speeds are good for juicing soft fruits such as grapes, and the high speed is better for firmer vegetables such as carrots and sweet potatoes.

Storage and cord length

Look for a model with a long cord to give you greater flexibility in terms of where it can be placed on your counter when juicing. If you plan to store your juicer in your cupboard, make sure you choose one that fits as they tend to take up room.

Value

You get what you pay for when it comes to juicers. Less expensive juicers tend to yield less juice, which will actually cost you more in the long run since you'll have to buy more produce to get enough juice into your glass. On the other hand, you don't need to go out and spend an arm and a leg for a top-of-the-line juicer. For most of us, something in the middle – around £100 to £180 – is just about right.

Making Juice, Step by Step

You have your juicer, so now what? You juice!

1. **Wash produce thoroughly.** Unwashed fruit and vegetables can be coated with dirt or bacteria, so a quick wash is an important step in the juicing process.
2. **Peel if necessary.** Peeling lemons and limes is optional,

but I typically peel oranges and grapefruits (more on that later).

3. **Cut or tear produce to size.** It must be able to fit through the juicer's feeder tube, so cut any produce that might be too large to fit.

4. **Feed produce through the juicer's chute.** If your machine has more than one speed, you can shift from high for harder produce such as apples and cucumbers, to low for softer fruits and vegetables such as spinach and berries.

That's it! You've made juice!

A few additional helpful tips:

- **Line your juicer's pulp basket with a plastic bag.** If your juicer has a pulp basket, lining the container makes washing-up easy. Look for bio-degradable bags that you can throw straight into the compost along with your pulp.

- **Fresh is best.** If you prefer your juice colder, pour over ice, but whatever the case, drink it as soon as possible because once it's juiced, it starts to lose its nutritional value. (See our next tip if you are making more than one at a time.)

- **Storing juice.** Stored properly, juice can last for two to three days, but remember that there are no preservatives in fresh juice (which is why we love it), so it can quickly go bad. To store it well, fill a glass jar to the very top, seal it right away and store in the refrigerator for up to 72 hours. Do not use metal storage containers, since metal can react with the acids in juice. You can also freeze your juice for up to ten days.

- **Clean your juicer after each use.** Scrub the machine with warm water and soap, and place on a drying rack. If your juicer's parts are dishwasher safe (check the manual), you'll have an even easier clean-up.
- **Consider re-using the pulp.** Visit our website www.rebootwithjoe.com to see the many ways you can use your leftover juice pulp. One idea is to use your vegetable pulp to make vegetable stock. You'll find the recipe on page 127.

Choosing the Best Produce

For your 5-Day Reboot, we've provided a detailed shopping list for the whole five days. Follow these guidelines to make your next visit to the farmers' market or grocery store quick, easy and affordable.

1. **Bright is best.** Always select the fruits and vegetables that are brightest in colour. If something is greying and discoloured, it might indicate spoiling.
2. **Don't aim for perfection.** Wrinkled, bruised and cracked produce may indicate the produce is spoiling, but much of it can still be used. When you are juicing, this doesn't need to be a number one concern.

3. **Smell before you buy.** Our sense of smell can be the best indicator of freshness. If it smells bad, put it down.
4. **Dirt is your friend.** If produce is fresh off the farm it won't always look perfect. It may have a little dirt on it or might not be perfectly shaped but you will know it's fresh, when nutrients are at their highest.
5. **Shop the sales.** Remember you can substitute different greens for any of the greens in our recipes, so if spinach is reduced, buy a bunch of it.

Storing Produce at Home

Since you aren't making every single juice you need for your 5-Day Reboot all at once, you'll need to store the fruits and vegetables in your kitchen. How you store them can determine a longer or shorter shelf life, so to help you get the most life out of your produce, follow these simple tips:

1. **Refrigerate or not?** If you don't know which produce you should refrigerate and which you should store at room temperature, take note of how the shop you are buying from stores it; if the shop keeps something at room temperature, then so should you.
2. **Know your fruits.** If refrigerating, place fruits in the crisper. Keep fruits that produce ethylene, such as apples, cantaloupe, honeydew melons and tomatoes away from other fruits and vegetables (ethylene vapours can cause other produce to ripen/spoil more rapidly). Store other

fruits in large baskets or bowls on the countertop uncovered but away from sunlight and heat.

3. **Know your veggies.** If refrigerating, place veggies in the produce drawer to keep them fresh. Vegetables such as onions, radishes, carrots, broccoli, cauliflower, leafy greens and squash store best unwashed and in a storage container such as a BPA-free produce saver. Store herbs by cutting off the ends and placing what's left in a cup of water. Cover the top with a plastic bag.

4. **Wait to wash.** Don't rinse your fruits and vegetables prior to storing in the refrigerator. Washing these items adds water content, which will increase the rate of spoilage.

5. **Keep an eye on it.** If produce you typically store at room temperature starts to brown or become softer, place it in the freezer or fridge! The colder temperatures will slow the ripening process. You can also go ahead and add it to a juice (even if the recipe doesn't particularly call for that item).

To Peel or Not to Peel?

In general, the outer layers of fruits and vegetables often provide more nutrition than the food they protect. For example, one tablespoon of lemon peel contains double the amount of vitamin C and triple the amount of fibre of one wedge of lemon without the peel. (Source: United States Department of Agriculture.)

As a general rule of thumb, if you aren't using organic

it's best to peel. This will greatly reduce the pesticide residue that accompanies conventionally raised produce. For most items with edible skins, such as cucumbers, courgettes, apples, pears and stone fruits, it is not necessary to peel before juicing if you're using organic produce.

Peeling is optional for some other items as follows:

Citrus Peels

With smaller citrus fruits such as lemon and lime, I like to leave the peel on because it gives the juice a slightly bitter, sour taste. Peel them if you like sweeter juice.

With bigger citrus fruits such as oranges and grapefruit, I typically peel these. They are much larger so the bitter taste is stronger. Also, these peels contain some oils that can cause indigestion, so if that's a worry for you, I say leave the peels for your compost.

Hard Fruit Rinds

Leaving the harder rinds on fruit like watermelon, cantaloupe and pineapple does not alter the taste much, and some rinds even add a higher dose of nutrients. Watermelon rind, for example, is lower in sugar content than the flesh, and higher in potassium and dietary fibre. If you are throwing away the rind, not only are you discarding about 40 per cent of the fresh weight of the watermelon, you are losing a potent source of an amino acid, citrulline.

Root Vegetable Skins

I choose to peel root vegetables such as beetroots and sweet potatoes because removing the peel takes away the earthy taste that often comes when leaving them on.

There's no need to peel thin-skinned root vegetables like carrots and parsnips.

Setting Up Your Body for Success: 'Transition In' Tips

If you learn anything from me, let it be this: don't do what I did and pretend that the night before your Reboot is the last time you will ever see, taste or smell food again. I considered it my last supper and I did not hold back. What I should have done was exactly the opposite. I should have enjoyed a meal that complemented what I was about to embark on. One rich in fruits and vegetables, one without processed food and trans fats, and one that would make me feel energized after a good night's sleep.

Instead, I binged on junk because I was having an emotional panic about the food I was about to leave behind. I was about to walk away from foods that had comforted me my whole life and I felt like I needed to say my goodbyes. Goodbyes are never easy but I guarantee they are a whole lot easier when you make the dietary changes recommended in preparing for your Reboot. Trying some of these 'transition in' tips in the week leading up to your Reboot will ease your body and mind into your 5-Day juicing adventure. I promise you, this part is so worth it.

One Week Before the Reboot

1. Refrain from eating processed 'junk' foods, white flour, sugar, desserts and fried foods.
2. Eliminate fast food and processed meats, such as bacon, ham and salami.
3. Put away the wine, beer and spirits for now.
4. Cut back on animal proteins. When you do eat them, choose wild-caught organic fish and organic eggs. Gradually decrease poultry consumption during the week. If you eat red meat, choose only lean cuts, and don't eat any meat past Day 3 of the preparation week. By the last day of this week, your protein should derive solely from plant sources, such as beans, nuts and legumes (e.g. chickpeas, lentils, almonds).
5. Cut back on dairy. Choose organic low-fat or non-fat dairy produce with little or no added sugars. If you opt for soy, rice or almond milk, choose the unflavoured and unsweetened types to limit the sugar content. By the end of the week, all dairy should be out of your diet.
6. Reduce caffeine little by little each day. Start substituting decaffeinated coffee for half of your daily consumption, or switch to green tea and then herbal tea.
7. Stay hydrated. Drink at least 1.5 litres (48 oz) per day, or aim for 2 litres (64 oz) if you are overweight, active, live in a warm climate or have a very physically demanding job.
8. Get extra sleep.

9. Practise using your juicer. Add at least one juice to your daily intake each day even if it's in addition to your other meals.
10. Up the plant foods. Start eating more salads, soups, smoothies and whole grains, along with nuts, seeds, natural nut butters, beans and legumes for protein.

The Day Before Your Reboot

1. Stop all non-prescription vitamins and supplements during the Reboot unless a doctor has advised you to take them. You're likely to be consuming a lot more nutrients than ever before, and if you're also taking vitamins and supplements, you might end up with more than the recommended daily allowance. Don't take any self-prescribed, over-the-counter medications.
2. Organize your shopping list and buy all the produce required for your 5-Day Reboot.
3. Drink at least one juice, and keep your meals free of meat, dairy and processed foods.

This is it. You now have all of the foolproof, simple tools you need to get through your 5-Day Reboot. Consider your start date, work on setting up the environment, get your kitchen ready for a juicer and an overflow of fruits and vegetables, and start gradually changing your diet so you're prepared mentally, physically and emotionally. These five days are going to change your life.

Chapter 7
Lift-Off!
Your 5-Day Plan

This is it! You're prepped, primed and raring to go. The plan is simple: you'll be drinking five juices per day, plus coconut water, vegetable broth and/or herbal tea. If you're opting for the juice + dinner option, you'll be drinking three juices per day, plus a healthy plant-based dinner, along with coconut water, broth and/or tea.

Each day starts the same. A typical day on your Reboot looks like this:

WAKE UP: 250 ml/8 oz warm water with juice of 1 lemon. Wait 30 minutes before having your breakfast juice.

Starting your day with warm water and lemon gets you off to a healthy start. Drinking warm beverages in the morning can help with hydration and promote bowel regularity, plus lemon contains antioxidants and anti-inflammatory compounds.

BREAKFAST: 475 ml–600 ml/16–20 oz juice

Don't forget to drink your breakfast juice. You'll need the nutrients to give you energy to get you through your morning.

MID-MORNING: 475 ml/16 oz unsweetened coconut water or 250ml/8 oz organic vegetable stock.

Drinking electrolyte-rich fluids such as coconut water (choose unsweetened) or stock (choose regular, not low sodium, organic vegetable broth) can help to provide the important nutrients you need like sodium, potassium and magnesium, which may in turn help to prevent or lessen common symptoms that you may experience, including headaches, lethargy or dizziness. These are often linked to the drastic decrease in electrolyte intake compared to the typical Western diet where sodium consumption is tremendous.

LUNCH: 475 ml–600 ml/16–20 oz juice

A juicy lunch helps to fuel your system with a boost of nutrients.

MID-AFTERNOON: 475 ml–600 ml/16–20 oz juice

Forget the coffee; your juice will be the perfect snack to get you through the afternoon slump.

DINNER: Juice Only: 475 ml–600 ml/16–20 oz *or* Juice + Dinner: Reboot Dinner Recipe

No matter what option you choose, dinner will be a plant-based powerhouse.

EVENING SNACK: Juice Only: 475 ml–600 ml/16–20 oz juice *or* Juice + Dinner: 250 ml/8 oz herbal tea or vegetable broth

If you have eaten dinner, an evening juice isn't necessary, so stick with herbal teas or veggie broth, but if you're juicing only, add in the extra juice to continue to fuel your body so tomorrow you will wake up on the right foot.

ALL DAY: Stay hydrated.

Although you'll be drinking lots of juice, your body still needs plain water to help flush toxins and keep you regular. Each day, aim to drink at least 1.5 litres/48 oz of water in addition to your juice, broth and coconut water.

If you live in a hot climate, have a physically demanding job, exercise more than 30 minutes per day, or are a taller person, aim to drink 2 litres/64 oz per day. Drink plain filtered water. Once in a while, it's fine to enjoy sparkling water.

Substitutions

I want to encourage you to give all the recipes a try, even if they contain ingredients you think you don't like, or haven't tried. For example, eating a yellow pepper is very different from drinking one; the flavour of the juice is much sweeter than you might expect.

If you have an allergy, a condition that forces you to avoid certain ingredients, or if you really don't like a certain fruit or vegetable, we've included a substitution chart in Extras (page 148) to help you swap different ingredients.

Swap Your Greens

We know that finding certain greens may be a challenge depending on the season and where you live, so in our recipes you will see a recommended green that we think is best in the recipe, but you are welcome to choose any other greens. You can choose between kale, chard, romaine lettuce, spinach and greens, depending on what's available at your market, what looks the freshest and what's reduced in price.

If you have a thyroid condition, you may wish to avoid consuming raw cruciferous vegetables like kale and greens. You can always substitute spinach, chard or romaine lettuce.

While they may seem convenient, avoid those bags of pre-washed, packaged greens. That's because there are no stems! The stems give you a terrific amount of juice and nutrients, so it's better to buy bunches of greens that include the stems.

Opposite is a list of greens, their nutritional benefits, and equivalents should you choose to swap them for a different leafy green.

Family Add-Ons

For those choosing the dinner option, we've given you guidelines for making a family-friendly meal. Simply make the recipe, and if you prefer, add one of the suggested proteins for your family. We suggest beans/legumes from BPA-free cans (or cooked from dried), wild-caught fish, organic pasture-raised eggs and poultry and grass-fed beef. Choosing

	Romaine (Cos) Lettuce	Spinach	Kale (Tuscan Cabbage)	Chard (Silverbeet)	Greens (spring/collard)
NUTRIENTS	Calcium, omega-3s, vitamin C, iron and B vitamins Thyroid-friendly!	Vitamins A, C and E. A good source of calcium, iron, potassium, protein and choline Thyroid-friendly!	Vitamins A, B6, K and C, plus a good source of iron, calcium and electrolyte potassium	Vitamins A and C, plus a source of iron, and electrolytes magnesium, potassium and sodium Thyroid-friendly!	Vitamins A, C and E, beta-carotene and manganese.
TIPS	Produces the most juice and is a healthier choice than other common lettuce greens like iceberg and butter lettuce	If you're in a rush, spinach isn't the quickest choice as it's tough to clean and the pre-packaged kind doesn't offer much juice	Leaves provide the least amount of juice, so choose kale with long, thick stems	Often makes more juice than kale due to chard's thick, juicy stems	Ties with chard for juice yield. Choose bunches with large leaves and long stems
FOR AN EQUIVALENT AMOUNT OF JUICE, USE:	8 large leaves	60g/2 oz/2 cups with stems	6 stalks with stems	4 stalks with stems	4 stalks with stems

organic meat, fish and eggs, when possible, may limit your exposure to contaminants, GMOs and antibiotics used in the production of conventional animal products.

YOUR SHOPPING LIST

Now for the fun part: shopping for all those amazing fruits and vegetables. Here's your juice-only list, plus a separate list for those of you choosing the juice + dinner plan.

Juice Only List

VEGETABLES	FRUIT
27 carrots	9 lemons
3 sweet yellow (bell) peppers (capsicums)	3 limes
13 cucumbers	1.5 kg/3 lb/6 cups fresh or frozen pineapple
3 heads romaine (cos) lettuce	20 large apples (any variety)
8 large sweet potatoes	8 oranges
4 large beetroots (beets)	300 g/11 oz/2 cups red or black grapes
2 heads of celery	1 small pink or ruby grapefruit
2 bunches of parsley (about 6 oz/3 cups leaves)	5 pears
1 large bunch of spinach (about 6 oz/6 cups)	15 cm/6 in piece of fresh root ginger
1 head red cabbage	**GROCERIES**
1 large bunch of chard (silverbeet)	2.25 litres/80 oz coconut water
1 bunch of kale (Tuscan cabbage)	Sparkling water, plain and unsweetened (optional)
1 small cauliflower	1 litre/32 oz organic vegetable stock (optional)

Juice + Dinner List

2.25 litres/80 oz coconut water

VEGETABLES	
28 carrots	1 large bunch of chard (silverbeet)
3 sweet yellow (bell) peppers (capsicums)	1 large bunch of kale (Tuscan cabbage)
4 sweet green (bell) peppers (capsicums)	1 small cauliflower
3 sweet red (bell) peppers (capsicums)	5 large sweet potatoes
2 jalapeño peppers (optional)	3 yellow onions
12 cucumbers	3 red onions
3 heads of romaine (cos) lettuce	4 large tomatoes
2 large beetroots (beet)	1 head of broccoli
2 heads of celery	150 g/5 oz/2 cups mushrooms (any type)
2 bunches of parsley (about 6 oz/3 cups leaves)	1 large or 2 small courgettes (zucchini)
1 large bunch of spinach (about 6 oz/6 cups)	250 g/9 oz/2 cups green beans (fresh or frozen)
1 head of red cabbage	500 g/18 oz/3 cups corn kernels (fresh or frozen)

FRUIT	GROCERIES
8 lemons	475 ml/16 oz/2 cups organic vegetable stock (more if you plan to drink broth during the day or evening)
1 lime	
500 g/1 lb/2 cups fresh or frozen pineapple	
15 large apples (any variety)	4 x 400 g/14 oz cans organic diced tomatoes
4 oranges	Olive oil
300 g/11 oz/2 cups red or black grapes	Garlic
5 pears	Chilli powder
15 cm/6 in piece of fresh root ginger	Cumin
	Apple cider vinegar or balsamic vinegar
	Honey (optional)
	Tamari
	Sea salt
	Black pepper

DAY 1

The first day of a Reboot is usually a great day because of the excitement of starting your healthy new venture! You may feel tired if you are accustomed to drinking a lot of caffeine, so don't forget to drink your juice to stay energized. If you find you're really struggling, try a cup of green tea.

On Day 1 you may notice an energy-level decrease earlier in the evening so plan to get to bed early as sleep is essential for supporting the immune system and metabolism. Throughout the day, sipping on juices and other suggested fluids frequently is a helpful strategy to keep hunger, cravings and fatigue at bay.

Sugar cravings might creep up on you today, so we've included some great sweeter juices to keep you satisfied.

DAY 1 AT A GLANCE

DAY 1	Juice Only	Juice + Dinner
WAKE UP	250 ml/8 oz hot water with juice of 1 lemon	250 ml/8 oz hot water with juice of 1 lemon
BREAKFAST	Sunshine in a Glass	Sunshine in a Glass
MID-MORNING	475 ml/16 oz coconut water or 250 ml/8 oz vegetable broth	475 ml/16 oz coconut water or 250 ml/8 oz vegetable broth
LUNCH	Hawaiian Tropic Green Juice	Hawaiian Tropic Green Juice
MID-AFTERNOON	Sunshine in a Glass (second portion)	Sunshine in a Glass (second portion)
DINNER	Hawaiian Tropic Green Juice (second portion)	Reboot Chilli
EVENING	Creamy Orange Juice (first portion)	250 ml/8 oz herbal tea or vegetable broth
ADDITIONAL WATER	1.5–2 litres/48–64 oz	1.5–2 litres/48–64 oz

Tips for the day:

- Thaw your fruit if using frozen, either overnight in the fridge or by running under warm water.

- If using fresh organic pineapple, no need to peel but if it's not organic, peel before juicing.

- We recommend removing apple seeds before juicing. The seeds contain a small amount of toxic cyanide. You'd have to eat about 150 apple seeds to feel an effect, but all the same, I like to core my apples.

- If you're not crazy about coconut water, add lemon, orange or lime slices.

- For those doing the dinner option, freeze the second portion of your lunch-time juice. After these five days, you'll have five juices ready to go.

- For those doing just juice, refrigerate the second portion of your evening juice; you'll use it tomorrow.

- If you're doing the dinner plan, save 150 g/5 oz/2 cups of your chilli for your dinner on Day 3. Leftover chilli freezes well, so don't worry if you and your family don't finish it all.

DAY 1 RECIPES

Sunshine in a Glass

Makes 2 servings (475–600 ml/16–20 oz/2–2½ cups each)
Nutrition per serving: 187 kCal; 3 g protein; 0 g fat; 35 g carbohydrates;
2 g fibre; 26 g sugars; 99 mg sodium

- 2 oranges
- 1 apple
- 7 carrots
- 3 sweet yellow (bell) peppers (capsicums)
- 2.5 cm/1 in piece of fresh root ginger or ½ tsp dried
  ginger

1. Rinse all the produce. Cut the skin off the oranges,
   but leave as much white pith as you can.

2. Core and seed the apple.

3. Chop everything as necessary to fit the juicer.

4. Juice all the ingredients.

Hawaiian Tropic Green Juice

Makes 2 servings (475–600 ml/16–20 oz/2–2½ cups each)
Nutrition per serving: 122 kCal; 3 g protein; 0 g fat; 31 g carbohydrates; 0 g fibre; 16 g sugars; 10 mg sodium

375 g/13 oz/1½ cups fresh or frozen pineapple (thawed)
1 lime
1 apple
3 cucumbers
8 leaves romaine (cos) lettuce

1. Peel the pineapple if not organic. If using frozen pineapple, thaw overnight in the refrigerator, or place under running warm water. Peel the lime.

2. Rinse all the other produce. Core and seed the apple.

3. Chop everything as necessary to fit the juicer.

4. Juice all the ingredients.

Creamy Orange Juice

Makes 2 servings (475-600 ml/16-20 oz/2-2½ cups each)
Nutrition per serving: 541 kCal; 6 g protein; 1 g fat; 108 g carbohydrates;
5 g fibre; 16 g sugars; 10 mg sodium

4 apples
2 oranges
3 sweet potatoes
6 carrots
dash of ground cinnamon

1. Rinse all the produce. Core and seed the apples.

2. Cut the skin off the oranges, but leave as much white pith as you can.

3. Chop everything as necessary to fit the juicer.

4. Juice all the ingredients.

5. Stir in the cinnamon.

Reboot Chilli

Makes 4 servings (about 225 g/8 oz/3 cups each)

Nutrition per serving (not including Family Add-on): 430 kCal; 16 g protein; 14 g fat; 1 g saturated fat; 66 g carbohydrates; 5 g fibre; 30 g sugar; 1909 mg sodium

Preparation: 15 minutes

Cooking: 25 minutes

- 4 tbsp olive oil
- 2 onions, chopped
- 4 carrots, chopped
- 2 garlic cloves, crushed (minced)
- 2 sweet green (bell) peppers (capsicums), deseeded and chopped
- 2 sweet red (bell) peppers (capsicums), deseeded and chopped
- 2 jalapeño peppers (optional)
- 3 tbsp chilli powder
- 1 tbsp ground cumin
- 1 tsp sea salt
- 4 x 400 g/14 oz cans chopped (crushed) tomatoes, preferably organic
- 500 g/18 oz/3 cups corn kernels
- 950 ml/32 oz/4 cups organic vegetable stock
- 16 kale (Tuscan cabbage) leaves, chopped, and stems chopped separately

Optional Family Add-on per person: Serve with 75 g/3 oz/½ cup cooked beans or legumes, or 75 g/3 oz cooked chicken, turkey or beef.

1. Place the oil in a large saucepan over a medium heat. Add the onions and carrots and cook until they begin to soften, about 4 minutes. Add the garlic and cook for another 3 minutes.

2. Add the sweet (bell) peppers (capsicums) and jalapeño, if using.

3. Sprinkle in the spices and salt, then stir to combine.

4. Add the tomatoes, corn and stock. Bring to the boil, then simmer for 10 minutes, or until the vegetables are cooked.

5. Stir in the kale (Tuscan cabbage) leaves and cook until they wilt, about 5 minutes.

6. Ladle into bowls, adding the extra family protein, if using.

7. Reserve 225 g/8 oz/3 cups of chilli for your Day 3 dinner.

DAY 1 WRAP UP

You did it! You started and completed Day 1 of your 5-Day plan. You're 20 per cent there! You might be feeling a little achy, or tired, but you should also be feeling 100 per cent PROUD.

Take a moment to note how you felt today, physically and mentally.

DAY 2

Congratulations on your first day of juicing! Today, we have some powerful antioxidants lined up for your juicing pleasure. Day 2 is traditionally the most challenging. You are likely to wake up feeling tired and may have a bit of a headache. Don't fret! Stick to your juicing schedule and be sure to stay well hydrated. Your electrolyte-rich coconut water and/or stock can help to recharge your day. Plan to take it easy and don't overschedule (not always possible, I know!).

DAY 2 AT A GLANCE

DAY 2	Juice Only	Juice + Dinner
WAKE UP	250 ml/8 oz hot water with juice of 1 lemon	250 ml/8 oz hot water with juice of 1 lemon
BREAKFAST	Sunrise Juice	Sunrise Juice
MID-MORNING	475 ml/16 oz coconut water or 250 ml/8 oz vegetable stock	475 ml/16 oz coconut water or 250 ml/8 oz vegetable stock
LUNCH	Herby Green Juice	Herby Green Juice
MID-AFTERNOON	Sunrise Juice (second portion)	Sunrise Juice (second portion)
DINNER	Herb-y Green Juice (second portion)	Roasted Vegetables with Herbs
EVENING	Creamy Orange Juice (second portion from yesterday)	250 ml/8 oz herbal tea or vegetable stock
ADDITIONAL WATER	1.5–2 litres/48–64 oz	1.5–2 litres/48–64 oz

Tips for the day:

- You don't have to peel your beetroots – if you don't, your juice will have an earthier flavour. Go ahead and peel, and cut off the ends if you want to avoid that.

- You can use fresh ginger in your juice. If fresh isn't available, stir in dried ginger or cinnamon after juicing.

- We love fresh parsley in today's green juice, but feel free to substitute fresh mint, basil or coriander.

DAY 2 RECIPES

Sunrise Juice

Makes 2 servings (475–600 ml/16–20 oz/2–2½ cups each)

Nutrition per serving: 281 kCal; 6 g protein; 1 g fat; 67 g carbohydrates; 4 g fibre; 35 g sugars; 262 mg sodium

2 apples

8 carrots

2 beetroot (beets), peeled if desired

1 sweet potato

8 romaine (cos) lettuce leaves

2.5 cm/1 in piece of fresh ginger or ½ tsp dried ginger

1. Rinse all the produce. Core and seed the apples.

2. Chop everything as necessary to fit the juicer.

3. Juice all the ingredients.

Herby Green Juice

Makes 2 servings (16–20 oz/475–600 ml/2–2½ cups each)
Nutrition per serving: 99 kCal; 4 g protein; 1 g fat, 23 g carbohydrates; 1 g fibre; 13 g sugars; 105 mg sodium

1 apple
½ lemon (optional)
6 celery sticks
2 cucumbers
120 g/4½ oz/2 cups fresh parsley
60 g/2¼ oz/2 cups spinach

1. Rinse all the produce. Core and seed the apple. Peel the lemon, if desired.

2. Chop everything as necessary to fit the juicer.

3. Juice all the ingredients.

Roasted Vegetables with Herbs

Serves 2

Nutrition per serving (not including Family Add-on): 462 kCal; 18 g protein; 17 g fat; 2 g saturated fat; 73 g carbohydrates; 25 g fibre; 26 g sugar; 838 mg sodium

Preparation: 15 minutes

Cooking: 40 minutes

2 sweet potatoes

2 large tomatoes

1 large bunch broccoli (about 200 g/7 oz/3 cups of florets)

1 red onion

60 g/2¼ oz/1 cup parsley leaves, finely chopped

1 garlic clove, crushed (minced)

2 tbsp olive oil

½ tsp sea salt

¼ tsp black pepper

Optional Family Add-on per person: Serve with 75 g/3 oz/½ cup cooked beans or legumes, or 75 g/3 oz cooked fish, chicken, turkey or beef.

1. Preheat the oven to 200°C/400°F/gas 6.

2. Rinse and chop the vegetables. Put the sweet potatoes into a large bowl and toss with 1 tablespoon of the olive oil. Spread them on a baking tray and bake for 40 minutes.

3. Meanwhile, toss the remaining vegetables, parsley and garlic, with the remaining tablespoon of olive oil, plus the salt and pepper.

4. Arrange the vegetable mixture in another large baking tray and place in the oven for the last 20 minutes of the potatoes' cooking time, stirring once or twice. They are ready when tender and beginning to brown.

5. Combine all vegetables together and stir before serving.

6. Serve alongside Family Add-on, if using.

DAY 2 WRAP UP

You're two days into your Reboot, and you might not be feeling terrific, but don't panic! It will get better. Drastic changes to your daily schedule or diet, even healthy ones, can take some adjustment (or time to get used to). Take time to go slower, go for a walk and get to bed early. Tomorrow is a new day and you're on the road to feeling good!

Take a moment to note how you felt today, physically and mentally.

DAY 3

You've made it to 'halfway day!' You might be tempted to skip juices today, but you need all those nutrients, so don't even think about it.

Today is the day the fog may start to clear and your energy may start to improve. Your body may be going through the transition period where you're leaving the processed-food cravings behind and the desire for plant-based nutrients is stepping in. Be sure to stick to your schedule for juices, hydration and electrolytes. Skipping 'meals' will probably lead to a sharp decline in how well you're feeling.

Some people experience moving their bowels less (or more) during a juice-only Reboot. If this is the case – besides staying hydrated – add in some senna tea if constipated.

DAY 3 AT A GLANCE

DAY 3	Juice Only	Juice + Dinner
WAKE UP	250 ml/8 oz hot water with juice of 1 lemon	250 ml/8 oz hot water with juice of 1 lemon
BREAKFAST	Deep Purple Juice	Deep Purple Juice
MID-MORNING	475 ml/16 oz coconut water or 250 ml/8 oz vegetable stock	475 ml/16 oz coconut water or 250 ml/8 oz vegetable stock
LUNCH	Love Those Leafy Greens	Love Those Leafy Greens
MID-AFTERNOON	Deep Purple Juice (second portion)	Deep Purple Juice (second portion)
DINNER	Love Those Leafy Greens (second portion)	Reboot Chilli (leftovers from Day 1)
EVENING	Sweet Beet	250 ml/8 oz herbal tea or vegetable stock
ADDITIONAL WATER	1.5–2 litres/48–64 oz	1.5–2 litres/48–64 oz

Tips for the day:

- Cabbage is packed with nutrients, but don't worry! Your juice won't taste like sauerkraut. Take this time to enjoy some new flavours. Cabbage is also the most nutrient-dense vegetable for your money.

- Peeling your lemons before juicing is optional. Leaving on the skin will give your juices more of a lemon flavour but also more bitterness, so if that bothers you, peel the top yellow layer off, leaving as much of the white pith as possible (it's highly nutritious, and so are the peels).

- Be aware that grapefruit can interfere with certain medications, including statins for high cholesterol. If your doctor or pharmacist has advised you to avoid grapefruit, you can substitute oranges for the grapefruit in your evening juice.

DAY 3 RECIPES

Deep Purple Juice

Makes 2 servings (475–600 ml/16–20 oz/2½ cups each)
Nutrition per serving: 197 kCal; 4 g protein; 1 g fat; 50 g carbohydrates; 2 g fibre; 35 g sugars; 34 mg sodium

    2 apples
    ½ head of red cabbage (if avoiding raw brassicas, use
        3 large beetroot (beets) instead)
    300 g/11 oz/2 cups red or black grapes
    8 romaine (cos) lettuce leaves

1. Rinse all the produce. Core and seed the apples. Stem the grapes.

2. Chop everything as necessary to fit the juicer.

3. Juice all the ingredients.

Love Those Leafy Greens

Makes 2 servings (475–600 ml/16–20 oz/2½ cups each)

Nutrition per serving: 202 kCal; 8 g protein; 1 g fat; 49 g carbohydrates; 1 g fibre; 29 g sugars; 2 g sodium

- 1 lemon
- 3 apples
- 16 romaine (cos) lettuce leaves
- 16 chard (silverbeet) leaves, including stems (if avoiding raw brassicas, use spinach instead, or add more lettuce)
- 1 large cucumber

1. Rinse all the produce. Peel the lemon if desired. Core and seed the apples.

2. Chop everything as necessary to fit the juicer.

3. Juice all the ingredients.

Sweet Beetroot

Makes 1 serving (475–600 ml/16–20 oz/2½ cups)
Nutrition per serving: 343 kCal; 8 g protein; 1 g fat; 80 g carbohydrates; 5 g fibre; 42 g sugars; 303 mg sodium

2 oranges
2 large beetroot (beets)
1 sweet potato

1. Rinse all the produce. Peel the oranges, leaving as much white pith as possible. Peel the beetroot, if desired.

2. Chop everything as necessary to fit the juicer.

3. Juice all the ingredients.

DAY 3 WRAP UP

Keep up with your healthy habits and get to bed early. Consider preparing your juices the night before to help stay on track in the busy morning rush out the door.

Most Reboot participants start to notice big changes after the third day. Their energy level is up, the unwanted symptoms like fatigue and headaches begin to subside, and they get a glimpse of what their healthier selves look like. Don't stop now – it's all worth it.

Take a moment to note how you felt today, physically and mentally.

DAY 4

Welcome to Day 4! You're probably finding that you're craving veggies! Your body may be adjusting to the increase in fluid intake, hopefully meaning fewer trips to the bathroom. Walking is a wonderful way to help promote bowel regularity, support immunity and metabolism, and is a perfect addition to juicing. Get out and go for a walk – 5 minutes, 10 minutes, 30 or more; the goal is to get moving but not push it too hard.

You are most probably starting to feel really good today. You may notice your brain fog is gone, your skin has that glowing look, and your sugar cravings have subsided, or at least quietened. These are just some of the benefits of juicing!

DAY 4 AT A GLANCE

DAY 1	Juice Only	Juice + Dinner
WAKE UP	250 ml/8 oz hot water with juice of 1 lemon	250 ml/8 oz hot water with juice of 1 lemon
BREAKFAST	Veggie Champagne	Veggie Champagne
MID-MORNING	475 ml/16 oz coconut water or 250 ml/8 oz vegetable stock	475 ml/16 oz coconut water or 250 ml/8 oz vegetable stock
LUNCH	Your Daily Green	Your Daily Green
MID-AFTERNOON	Veggie Champagne (second portion)	Veggie Champagne (second portion)
DINNER	Your Daily Green (second portion)	Reboot Super Salad
EVENING	Citrus Refresher	250 ml/8 oz herbal tea or vegetable broth
ADDITIONAL WATER	1.5–2 litres/48–64 oz	1.5–2 litres/48–64 oz

Tips for the day:

- Cauliflower is a great juicing ingredient. It's a high-yield vegetable (meaning you get a lot of juice), and the flavour is mild and sweet. Be sure to juice the stems, too.

- Fresh ginger has terrific health benefits, and we use it in a lot of recipes. But if you can't find it or don't like it, substitute lemon or add dried ginger after juicing.

- Try to get moving today: a 20- or 30-minute walk benefits the whole body and mind.

DAY 4 RECIPES

Veggie Champagne

Makes 2 servings (475–600 ml/16–20 oz/2–2½ cups each)
Nutrition per serving: 155 kCal; 4 g protein; 1 g fat; 38 g carbohydrates; 3 g fibre; 23 g sugars; 118 mg sodium

½ small head of cauliflower (if avoiding raw brassicas, use 4 large parsnips instead)
8 celery sticks
3 pears
5 cm/2 in piece of fresh root ginger or ½ tsp dried ginger
1 cucumber
sparkling water (optional)

1. Rinse all the produce.

2. Chop everything as necessary to fit the juicer.

3. Juice all the ingredients.

4. For a little fizz, top up your juice with a splash of sparkling water.

Your Daily Green

Makes 2 servings (475–600 ml/16–20 oz/2–2½ cups each)
Nutrition per serving: 177 kCal; 4 g protein; 1 g fat; 45 g carbohydrates; 2 g fibre; 34 g sugars; 77 mg sodium

1 lemon
3 apples
3 cucumbers
5 celery sticks
60 g/2¼ oz/1 cup parsley, with stems

1. Rinse all the produce. Peel the lemon if desired. Core and seed the apples.

2. Chop everything as necessary to fit the juicer.

3. Juice all the ingredients.

Citrus Refresher

Makes 1 serving (475–600 ml/16–20 oz/2–2½ cups)

Nutrition per serving: 391 kCal; 6 g protein; 1 g fat; 98 g carbohydrates; 3 g fibre; 52 g sugars; 181 mg sodium

1 kg/2 lb 4oz/4 cups fresh or frozen pineapple (thawed)

1 sweet potato

4 celery sticks

1 lemon

1 lime

sparkling water (optional)

1. Rinse all the produce. Peel the pineapple if not organic. If using frozen pineapple, thaw overnight in the refrigerator, or place under running warm water. Peel the lime and lemon (optional).

2. Chop everything as necessary to fit the juicer.

3. Juice all the ingredients.

4. If you want to add a little fizz, top up your juice with a splash of sparkling water.

Reboot Super Salad

Serves 2

Nutrition per serving (not including Family Add-on): 407 kCal; 6 g protein; 28 g fat; 4 g saturated fat; 40 g carbohydrates; 10 g fibre; 26 g sugar; 341 mg sodium

Preparation: 15 minutes

200 g/7 oz/4 cups romaine (cos) lettuce leaves, torn
1 large tomato, chopped
1 sweet red (bell) pepper (capsicum), deseeded and chopped
½ red onion, diced
1 cucumber, diced
1 tomato, diced
1 carrot, peeled and grated
1 apple, diced
5 oz/150 g/2 cups mushrooms, sliced

For the dressing
4 tbsp olive oil
1 tsp apple cider or balsamic vinegar
1 garlic clove, crushed (minced)
1 tablespoon parsley leaves, chopped
½ tsp honey (optional)
sea salt and freshly ground pepper to taste

Optional Family Add-on per person: Serve with 75 g/3 oz/½ cup cooked beans or legumes, or 2 hard-boiled eggs, or 75 g/3 oz/ cooked fish, chicken, turkey or beef.

1. Rinse all the produce.

2. Combine all vegetables and the apple in a large bowl.

3. Put the dressing ingredients into a small bowl and whisk together.

4. Pour the dressing over the salad and toss well.

5. Top with Family Add-on, if using.

DAY 4 WRAP UP

Continue to get to bed early and prep your juices for the next day. Making healthy eating a sustainable system that fits into your everyday life is key to maintaining the behaviours and benefits you may have experienced so far.

It's the home stretch! That means it's time to think about what you'll do after these five days are over. Check out Chapter 8 to learn how to turn these five days into the start of a lifetime of health.

Take a moment to note how you felt today, physically and mentally.

DAY 5

Today you may wake up feeling ready to tackle the world and thinking that juicing is pretty awesome. You may even want to continue juicing after these five days! We do suggest including at least one fresh juice as a daily nutrient-dense addition to your life. Adding in fresh juice once a day to a meal, or even in place of a meal for some individuals, is a healthy strategy to promote wellness and weight management.

Enjoy feeling energized and confident in your ability to bypass those workplace pastries, and savour the pleasure of knowing you're fuelling your body with nutrients and experimenting with new flavours and foods.

DAY 5 AT A GLANCE

DAY 1	Juice Only	Juice + Dinner
WAKE UP	250 ml/8 oz hot water with juice of 1 lemon	250 ml/8 oz hot water with juice of 1 lemon
BREAKFAST	I'm Seeing Red	I'm Seeing Red
MID-MORNING	475 ml/16 oz coconut water or 250 ml/8 oz vegetable stock	475 ml/16 oz coconut water or 250 ml/8 oz vegetable stock
LUNCH	Easy Being Green	Easy Being Green
MID-AFTERNOON	I'm Seeing Red (second portion)	I'm Seeing Red (second portion)
DINNER	Easy Being Green (second portion)	Veggie Stir-fry with Cauliflower Rice
EVENING	Grapefruit Punch	250 ml/8 oz herbal tea or vegetable broth
ADDITIONAL WATER	1.5–2 litres/48–64 oz	1.5–2 litres/48–64 oz

Tips for the day:

- Don't neglect to juice the stems of your greens: you get more juice from the stems than from the leaves.

- Left-over greens or veggies from the week? Toss them in!

- Check our website for juicer-pulp recipes, www.rebootwithjoe.com

DAY 5 RECIPES

I'm Seeing Red

Makes 2 servings (475–600 ml/16–20 oz/2–2½ cups each)
Nutrition per serving: 279 kCal; 5 g protein; 1 g fat; 66 g carbohydrates; 4 g fibre; 25 g sugars; 201 mg sodium

- ½ head of red cabbage (if avoiding raw brassicas, use 3 large beetroot (beets) instead)
- 6 carrots
- 2 oranges
- 2 sweet potatoes

1. Rinse all the produce. Peel the oranges, leaving as much white pith as possible.

2. Chop everything as necessary to fit the juicer.

3. Juice all the ingredients.

Easy Being Green

Makes 2 servings (475–600 ml/16–20 oz/2–2½ cups each)

Nutrition per serving: 171 kCal; 3 g protein; 0 g fat; 40 g carbohydrates; 4 g fibre; 19 g sugars; 36 mg sodium

- 120 g/4½ oz/4 cups spinach
- 8 kale (Tuscan cabbage) leaves with stalks (if avoiding raw brassicas, use romaine (cos) lettuce instead, or add more spinach)
- 2 apples
- 1 cucumber
- 2 pears
- 5 cm/2 in piece of fresh root ginger

1. Rinse all the produce. Core and seed the apples.

2. Chop everything as necessary to fit the juicer.

3. Juice all the ingredients.

Grapefruit Punch

Makes 1 serving (475-600 ml/16-20 oz/2-2½ cups)
Nutrition per serving: 199 kCal; 5 g protein; 1 g fat; 47 g carbohydrates; 2 g fibre; 33 g sugars; 18 mg sodium

   1 apple
   1 small red/ruby grapefruit (if this conflicts with your medications, use 2 oranges instead)
   1 lime
   8 kale (Tuscan cabbage) leaves and stalks (if avoiding raw brassicas, use romaine (cos) lettuce or spinach instead)
   2 cucumbers

1. Rinse all the produce. Core and seed the apple.

2. Peel the grapefruit and lime, leaving as much white pith as you can.

3. Chop everything as necessary to fit the juicer.

4. Juice all the ingredients.

Veggie Stir-fry with Cauliflower Rice

Serves 2

Nutrition per serving (not including Family Add-on): 300 kCal; 10 g protein; 15 g fat; 2 g saturated fat; 40 g carbohydrates; 17 g fibre; 20 g sugar; 450 mg sodium

Preparation: 15 minutes

Cooking: 15 minutes

½ head of cauliflower

2 tbsp olive oil

1 red onion, diced

2 carrots, sliced

2 garlic cloves, crushed (minced)

2 sweet green (bell) peppers (capsicums), deseeded and chopped

1 large or 2 small courgettes (zucchini), sliced

250 g/9 oz/2 cups green beans, fresh or frozen

2 tsp tamari

freshly ground black pepper, to taste

Optional Family Add-on per person: Serve with 75 g/3 oz/½ cup cooked beans or legumes, or 75 g/3 oz cooked fish, chicken, turkey or beef.

1. Rinse all the produce.

2. Remove the thick stem from the cauliflower. Roughly chop the remainder into florets.

3. Put the cauliflower into a steamer and steam for 8–10 minutes, until just tender. Transfer the florets to a food processor and pulse until the texture of rice.

4. Place the oil in a large frying pan (skillet) on a medium-high heat.

5. Add the onion and carrots, and sauté for about 5 minutes, or until the onions are translucent. Add the garlic and stir for another 2 minutes.

6. Add the sweet (bell) peppers (capsicums) and cook for 5 minutes.

7. Add the courgettes (zucchini) and green beans and continue cooking until all the vegetables are tender but still crisp, about 5 minutes.

8. Turn off the heat. Add the tamari and black pepper.

9. Serve with the cauliflower rice and Family Add-on, if using.

DAY 5 WRAP UP

You are well on your way to a plant-based lifestyle and healthy eating for the long haul. This is the end of an amazing commitment and journey, and the beginning of experiencing the incredible potential for a healthier, happier life.

You've taken the first five steps towards getting your health and weight management on track, with five days of delicious, plant-based nutrition. You've drastically cut the intensity of your sugar cravings, lessened the need for excess caffeine in your life and discovered that you truly can combat the late-night munchies. I'm so proud of you! The first five days of my 60-day Reboot were the hardest, but also the most rewarding, because I knew I could do it.

Give yourself a pat on the back and make the decision to continue improving your health. Head to Chapter 8 to choose a path, and congratulations!

Take a moment to note how you felt today, physically and mentally.

Chapter 8
Beyond Your Reboot

Here we are, you did it! Remember when you first opened this book and you had doubts? You thought, 'I don't know if I can do these five days; I've failed before, so why is this time going to be different?' But now you know. You know what it feels like to flood your body with essential nutrients that help it function at its optimal level, to feel energized, happy and on top of the world. You've discovered that you *do* have the power to improve your health, to take your place in the driver's seat and decide which road you want to take to not just live your life, but thrive.

I think back to when I completed my first Reboot. As you can see in my film *Fat, Sick & Nearly Dead*, I decided to take a hot air balloon ride. I was physically and mentally feeling on top of the world, so I figured, why not go there literally? I floated above the horizon feeling weightless. Nothing was holding me down, my mental clarity was beyond anything I had ever felt, and my energy was through the clouds. This was after 60 days of nothing but juice, but I reckon you're experiencing some of these same feelings after just five days. Take a minute to let this moment soak in, pat yourself on the back and feel accomplished. I am proud of you and you should be extremely proud of yourself.

There's nowhere to go but up at this point. You're likely to be feeling healthier and maybe you've lost a couple of pounds. You've witnessed first-hand what consuming plant foods can do for you and now you're determined to make them a part of your everyday life. And this is just the beginning. Unlike other weight loss attempts you've tried before that had a beginning and an end, this new way of life just keeps going. You're going to crave more fruits, vegetables and whole foods. You'll turn your nose up at processed foods. Now that you know what it feels like to actually nourish your body, and understand that's what you have needed all along, you won't want to stop after these five days. There are a few different ways you can move forward on this path. Read through them and decide on the best one for you. Everyone is different. There is no wrong way, but the right way is to do what is best for you, your health and your needs.

1. Keep Rebooting

If you're like me, once you get a dose of what it feels like to drink nothing but liquid sunshine all day long, then you might have the desire to keep going. You like Rebooting, you like the way it makes you feel, you like seeing the pounds slip off, and your trousers fitting a little easier.

Then go for it, and keep Rebooting. Many of those who've lost 30, 50, even 100 pounds through juicing started just like you did, with a five-day experiment. They loved the results they were seeing on a daily basis, so they'd juice for one more day, and then another, and before they knew it they were completing a 30-Day Reboot. If you find yourself on this same pattern and you decide to go beyond 15 days, we recommend that you seek supervision from a medical professional who will help monitor your medications and improving health, and determine any needs along the way.

Here are a couple of options to consider if you want to keep Rebooting:

- **Repeat this 5-Day Reboot.** Keep it easy. If you liked this 5-Day Reboot, repeat it! You can follow the exact same plan, use the same shopping list, follow the same guidelines, and you don't have to think about anything except turning on your juicer. If you have a desire for a little more variety, refer to our substitutions list on page 148 and experiment with other fruits and vegetables in your juices.

- **Try our other Reboot plans.** Our resources don't stop here. My first book, *The Reboot with Joe Juice Diet*, includes plans for 3-, 5-, 10-, 15- and 30-day Reboots that include juice only, or juicing and eating. *The Reboot with Joe Juice Diet Recipe Book* offers more recipes as well. If you need more inspiration in the kitchen, you can download our 101 Juice Recipes app to your iOS or

Android device to literally have juice recipes at your fingertips every day.

- If you'd like more assistance and nutritional guidance as you get closer to your goals, my website, www.rebootwithjoe.com features Guided Reboot programmes that are designed to do just that. With the help of a Reboot nutritionist, a Guided Reboot utilizes the knowledge, support and direction of the coaches to help you successfully reach your weight loss and health goals. Our Guided Reboots include 15-Day and 30-Day, along with two 60-Day programmes, one dedicated to help those with type-2 diabetes and the other for those with thyroid issues.

2. Transition Out of Your Reboot

If this 5-Day Reboot is exactly what you needed to gain the motivation and dedication to improve your diet, then maybe you've decided you're ready to start adding whole foods back into your day. If you choose this option, it doesn't mean you're less successful than someone who continues a Reboot for 20 days. You just need to make sure that you go about it the smart way and don't jump right back into old unhealthy ways of eating. If you've spent five hours cleaning your car making sure it's shiny and pristine, you aren't going to go and drive it through a muddy field, and you should look at your body the same way. Adding a burger and fries to a digestive system that's only consumed juices for the past five days would be quite a shock to your body. Give it time, ease back in and be patient.

Generally speaking, spend the first five days after your Reboot following a mostly-plants diet. This includes drinking fresh juice at least once or twice a day and vegetable or fruit-only meals and snacks.

You can return to eating three meals a day if that's what you're used to, but you should continue to have at least one juice a day. Juices make great snacks or a light breakfast. You should also continue to stay hydrated and drink lots of water, including hot water with lemon in the morning and herbal teas at night. Read on for more in-depth tips on transitioning out of your Reboot.

Transition Out of Your Reboot

The key to a lifetime of health goes well beyond completing one 5-Day Reboot. It's about making long-term changes to your diet and lifestyle. This starts with a successful transition out of your juice Reboot. If you want specific guidelines to follow for your next five days post-Reboot, read on. We've also provided Transition Recipes and a day-at-a-glance so there's no guessing about how you should approach this transition phase. Each day of your transition period will add in a new food group. Our recommendations are optional; make sure to only consume foods that are right for you.

A Reboot is a natural elimination diet, so the reason we

suggest adding foods back in slowly is to allow your body time to adjust to the foods you haven't been consuming for the past five days, and determine if there's a certain food group that causes digestive issues. For example, if you choose to add back grains with gluten and you get an upset stomach soon after, you may want to take note and lessen the amount of gluten you consume. The same goes for dairy products. Take it slowly and be sure to note how you feel after you consume newly introduced foods.

DAY AT A GLANCE

A typical day during your transition out period will look something like this:

Breakfast: Juice
Mid-Morning: Juice or Snack
Lunch: Salad or Entrée leftovers
Afternoon: Juice or Snack
Dinner: Entrée

Day 1

- Continue with water and fresh juices, consuming 2–3 juices per day of your choice.
- Add in 1–2 small meals and snacks as needed, consisting of raw, steamed, roasted, baked, grilled, stir-fried or sautéed fruits and vegetables, or a simple vegetable soup.

- Keep your portions small. Eat slowly and chew well.
- Continue to stay away from caffeine and added or refined sugars.

Day 2

- Continue with water and fresh juices, consuming 1–2 juices per day.
- Add in 2–3 small meals and snacks, consisting of raw, steamed, roasted, baked, grilled, stir-fried or sautéed fruits and vegetables, or a simple vegetable soup.
- You may add in gluten-free whole grains, including amaranth, buckwheat, millet, quinoa, rice, teff and certified gluten-free oats.
- If it feels right, add in another meal so that you're up to three small meals a day. Add healthy snacks as needed.
- Meals today can consist of juices, steamed, roasted and raw fruits and veggies, veggie soups and gluten-free whole grains.
- Continue to stay away from caffeine and added or refined sugars.

Day 3

- Continue with water and fresh juices, consuming 1–2 juices per day of your choice.
- You may add in seeds, nuts and beans. We recommend soaking and cooking dry beans or selecting canned beans

that are low in sodium and sold in BPA-free cans. Seeds and nuts should, ideally, be raw and not salted, roasted, candied, etc. Lightly roasted and/or salted nuts are acceptable in moderation.

- The added proteins and whole grains will give your body nutrients in a variety of forms and help to get you back to handling a regular, yet healthy and well-balanced diet.
- Add snacks in between meals as needed. Try fresh fruits and vegetables.
- Meals today can consist of juices, steamed, roasted and raw fruits and veggies, veggie soups, gluten-free whole grains, as well as nuts, seeds and beans.
- Continue to stay away from caffeine and added or refined sugars.

Day 4

- Continue with water and fresh juices, consuming 1–2 juices per day of your choice.
- Optionally, add in remaining whole grains if you do not wish to stay with just gluten-free grains. Grains with gluten include barley, whole wheat and all its varieties (spelt, kamut, faro, etc.) and rye.
- Meals today can consist of juices, steamed, roasted and raw fruits and veggies, veggie soups, whole grains, nuts, seeds and beans.
- Continue to stay away from caffeine and added or refined sugars.

Day 5

- Continue with water and fresh juices, consuming 1–2 juices per day of your choice.
- Choose to add organic, pasture-raised eggs and wild-caught fish if desired.
- Meals today can consist of juices, steamed, roasted and raw fruits and veggies, veggie soups, whole grains, nuts, seeds, beans and organic eggs or wild fish as desired.
- Slowly add in caffeinated teas such as green tea, if you wish.

Beyond Day 5

After a five-day transition period, continue to consume plenty of water and at least one juice per day in addition to a meal or as a meal or snack replacement. If you enjoy meat as part of your diet, now is the time you can start adding in organic poultry and grass-fed beef. You can also start adding in moderate amounts of organic dairy products, like plain Greek yogurt. If you do add in meat or dairy, keep portions light and small, while consuming higher amounts of plant-based foods.

Note that you may find yourself sensitive to some of the items you eliminated during the Reboot, so be sure to continue to take it slowly. If you find that low-fat dairy causes an upset stomach, limit it and replace it with a calcium-rich green juice or a vegetable snack rich in greens, like a kale salad. Most people find that post-Reboot, they experience a greater joy in eating more fruits and vegetables, and they continue to keep fresh juices in their diet. This is where the long-lasting and sustainable changes in your lifestyle begin to happen: eating a healthy well-balanced diet day after day.

Healthy Eating Tips to Take You Beyond Your Reboot

- Eat smaller amounts more often. This is essential for healthy digestion and continuing to manage appetite and ease food cravings. Eating just enough to nourish yourself without going beyond what is comfortable is at the heart of being gentle to your body.
- Consider how you cook your food to enhance the digestibility and nutrient value of your meals. Ideally, bake, grill, broil, roast and steam your food. Stir-frying is also acceptable if you use just a small amount of healthy oil, like olive or coconut. Avoid fried foods or anything with a lot of oil or added fats.
- Be very picky about the quality of your animal products. Local is best, when feasible. At the store, buy organic pasture-raised eggs, wild-caught fish, free-range organic chicken and grass-fed beef if you choose to consume them.
- Plan to include fresh juice and plenty of plant-based foods each and every day for optimal health and wellness.

How to Maintain Healthy Habits

Remember, we all get wet no matter how we jump into the swimming pool, so however you decide to complete your Reboot, the most important thing is that you learn to maintain the healthy habits you have built over the last five days.

In his book, *The Power of Habit*, the American writer Charles Duhigg brilliantly sums up how to look at habits. He writes: 'Most of the choices we make each day may feel like the products of well-considered decision making, but they're not. They're habits. And though each habit means relatively little on its own, over time, the meals we order, what we say to our kids each night, whether we save or spend, how often we exercise, and the way we organize our thoughts and work routines have enormous impacts on our health, productivity, financial security, and happiness. One paper published by a Duke University researcher in 2006 found that more than 40 percent of the actions people performed each day weren't actual decisions, but habits.'

So what does that mean for you? The more you incorporate healthier practices into your daily life, such as opting for a side salad instead of French fries, or fish and vegetables versus the pasta with cream sauce, the easier it is for you to stay committed to being healthy overall. These small changes are possible, even if it's something you've never done before.

In a 2008 *New York Times* article by Janet Rae-Dupree based on the research by M.J. Ryan, author of *This Year I Will*, Rae-Dupree writes: 'Rather than dismissing ourselves as unchangeable creatures of habit, we can instead direct our own change by consciously developing new habits. In fact, the more new things we try – the more we step outside our comfort zone – the more inherently creative we become, both in the workplace and in our personal lives. But don't bother trying to kill off old habits; once those ruts of procedure are worn into the hippocampus, they're there to stay. Instead, the new habits we deliberately ingrain into ourselves create parallel pathways that can bypass those old roads.'

So how can you generate change that's here to stay? Here's a start: focus on practising a lifestyle where at least 70 to 80 per cent of your choices are dedicated to healthy practices, and free up the other 20 to 30 per cent to enjoy a piece of chocolate cake, a glass of wine or a slice of pizza for dinner.

It's like having a budget. If you spent your entire salary on things you needed, such as your mortgage or rent, insurance, grocery store visits, and added some to your savings, then you wouldn't have anything left to afford a fun night out with friends. On the flip side, if you only spent your money on things you wanted, such as nice clothes, gourmet dinners and expensive holidays, well then your life needs wouldn't be met, you wouldn't be able to afford the roof over your head and the heating in your home would soon be turned off. Now if you take that salary and spend 80 per cent on your needs, and save 20 per cent for your wants, then you are living the best of both worlds. And that's how you should think about your lifestyle.

I believe a happy and healthy life is one with balance. If I was sitting here telling you to only drink juice for the rest of your life, well, that's not realistic. Instead of the saying 'Have your cake and eat it too', how about 'Have your juice and sometimes eat cake too'? That sounds like a good life motto.

To help you with maintaining healthy habits beyond this Reboot, we've provided you with a handful of transition recipes to complement your new diet. Enjoy this new life you've embarked on because not only are you changing your physical shape, you're changing your happiness, and I reckon, and I think we can all agree, that a happy, healthy life is what makes this world go round.

EXTRAS
Transition Recipes

Vegetable Broth

Makes 2 litres/64 oz/8 cups

Preparation: 15 minutes
Cooking: 30–120 minutes

1 tsp olive oil
500 g/16 oz/4 cups juice pulp (e.g. from Herby Green
  Juice recipe, page 000)
about 2.25 litres/64 oz/8 cups water
½ tsp sea salt
½ tsp freshly ground black pepper
fresh or dried herbs, e.g. basil, bay, chives, ginger,
  oregano, parsley, rosemary, thyme

1. Place the oil in a large saucepan over a medium heat.
   When hot, add the juice pulp. Stir and cook for 1–2
   minutes. Add the remaining ingredients and bring to
   the boil. Reduce the heat to medium, cover the pan
   and simmer for up to 2 hours. (For a quick version,
   cook uncovered for 20–30 minutes.)

2. Strain the stock, discarding the pulp. Allow to cool.

3. Pour the stock into glass or BPA-free plastic containers. Seal tightly and store in the refrigerator for up to 4 days, or in the freezer for 3 weeks.

JUICES

Pear Power Basil Juice

Makes 1 serving (475-600 ml/16-20 oz/2-2½ cups)
Nutrition per serving: 189 kCal; 3 g protein; 1 g fat; 48 g carbohydrates; 2 g fibre; 31 g sugars; 91 mg sodium

1 lemon
2 pears
4 celery sticks
1 cucumber
10 g/¼ oz/1 packed cup basil leaves

1. Rinse all the produce.

2. Peel the lemon, if desired.

3. Chop everything as necessary to fit the juicer.

4. Juice all the ingredients.

Sunny Citrus Beetroot Juice

Makes 1 serving (475–600 ml/16–20 oz/2–2½ cups)

Nutrition per serving: 200 kCal; 6 g protein; 1 g fat; 33 g carbohydrates; 1 g fibre; 33 g sugars; 55 mg sodium

1 lemon
1 small or ½ large grapefruit
2 beetroot (beets)
2 carrots

1. Rinse all the produce.

2. Peel the lemon, if desired.

3. Chop everything as necessary to fit the juicer.

4. Juice all the ingredients.

Greens and Carrot Juice

Makes 1 serving (475-600 ml/16-20 oz/2-2½ cups)

Nutrition per serving: 154 kCal; 2 g protein; 1 g fat; 36 g carbohydrates; 2 g fibre; 23 g sugars; 114 mg sodium

1 apple

½ lime

2 romaine (cos) lettuce leaves

3-4 sprigs of coriander (cilantro)

3-4 sprigs of parsley

4 carrots

1 in (2.5 cm) piece of fresh root ginger

1. Rinse all the produce. Core and seed the apple.

2. Peel the lime, if desired.

3. Chop everything as necessary to fit the juicer.

4. Juice all the ingredients.

Chard Rock Café Juice

Makes 1 serving (475-600 ml/16-20 oz/2-2½ cups)

Nutrition per serving: 94 kCal; 2 g protein; 0 g fat; 21 g carbohydrates; 1 g fibre; 23 g sugars; 223 mg sodium

½ lemon

3 carrots

1 cucumber

2 large chard (silverbeet) leaves

2 sprigs of fresh oregano or parsley

1. Rinse all the produce.

2. Peel the lemon, if desired.

3. Chop everything as necessary to fit the juicer.

4. Juice all the ingredients.

SNACKS

Red Pepper Sticks with Hummus

Serves 1

Nutrition per serving: 100 kCal; 4 g protein; 4 g fat; 14 g carbohydrates;
5 g fibre; 7 g sugars; 120 mg sodium

½ sweet red (bell) pepper (capsicum)
2 tbsp hummus

Slice the pepper into sticks and use for scooping up the
hummus.

Apple Almond

Serves 1

Nutrition per serving: 290 kCal; 7 g protein; 18 g fat; 2 g saturated fat; 31 g carbohydrates; 8 g fibre; 20 g sugars; 70 mg sodium

1 apple
2 tbsp almond butter

1. Core, seed and slice the apple.

2. Spread each slice with a thin layer of almond butter.

Mixed Nuts

Serves 1

Nutrition per serving: 220 kCal; 6 g protein; 20 g fat; 4 g saturated fat; 8 g carbohydrates; 2 g fibre; 72 g sugars; 110 mg sodium

35 g/1¼ oz/¼ cup raw mixed nuts (almonds, cashews, walnuts, etc.)

Weigh and mix your chosen combination of raw nuts.

LUNCH

Three-ingredient Kale Salad

Serves 4

Nutrition per serving: 370 kCal; 8 g protein; 30 g fat; 5 g saturated fat; 27 g carbohydrates; 5 g fibre; 7 g sugars; 230 mg sodium

Preparation: 15 minutes

Cooking: 3 minutes

16 leaves of fresh kale (Tuscan cabbage) or 8 oz/8 cups spinach leaves

70 g/2½ oz/½ cup toasted pine nuts or cashews

2 oranges, peeled and separated into segments

For the dressing

1 tsp Dijon mustard

2 tsp finely grated lemon zest

3 tbsp fresh lemon juice

6 tbsp extra virgin olive oil

sea salt and freshly ground black pepper

1. Separate the kale (Tuscan cabbage) leaves and discard the hard stems. Tear the leaves into bite-size pieces and place in a large bowl.

2. Put the nuts into a small frying pan (skillet) over a low heat and toast gently toast for 3 minutes, or until fragrant.

3. Combine the nuts and orange segments with the kale.

4. Put all the dressing ingredients into a small bowl and whisk together until thick and creamy.

5. Pour the dressing over the salad and toss well. Season with salt and pepper.

6. Chill before serving.

Egg and Avocado Mash

Serves 1

Nutrition per serving: 290 kCal; 13 g protein; 23 g fat; 9 g carbohydrates; 7 g fibre; 1 g sugars; 420 mg sodium

2 hard-boiled eggs
½ avocado
1 tsp fresh lemon juice
dash of red pepper flakes
sea salt and freshly ground black pepper

1. Chop the eggs and place them in a small bowl.

2. Add the avocado flesh, lemon juice and pepper flakes, then mash with a fork to whatever texture you prefer.

3. Season to taste.

4. Use the mash in a sandwich or a lettuce wrap, or as a dip.

Lentil and Quinoa Veggie Burgers

Serves 6

Nutrition per serving: 250 kCal; 13 g protein; 4 g fat; 41 g carbohydrates; 8 g fibre; 3 g sugars; 240 mg sodium

Preparation: 20 minutes, plus at least 4 hours chilling

Cooking: 20 minutes

90 g/3½ oz/½ cup uncooked quinoa

100 g/4 oz/1 cup dried red lentils

750 ml/24 oz/3 cups water, plus an extra 2½ tbsp

1 tbsp linseeds (flaxseed meal)

1 tsp olive oil

½ red onion, chopped

3 garlic cloves, crushed (minced)

½ tsp kosher salt, divided in two

2 tbsp tomato purée (paste)

1 sweet red (bell) pepper (capsicum), finely chopped

2 tbsp chopped coriander (cilantro)

1 dried chipotle chilli, crushed (minced)

2 tsp ground cumin

75 g/3 oz/½ cup rolled oats

25 g/1 oz/¼ cup oat flour

1. Place the quinoa and lentils in a small saucepan with the first quantity of water and bring to the boil. Lower the heat, cover the pan and cook for about 15 minutes, until the water is absorbed and the quinoa and lentils

are cooked. Set aside. (Note: this step can be done in advance.)

2. Meanwhile, combine the linseeds and the 2½ tablespoons of water, and set aside to soften.

3. Heat the oil in a small pan over a medium heat and add the onion and garlic. Add half the salt and sauté until the onions are softened, 5–6 minutes.

4. Transfer the mixture to a large bowl. Add the lentils and quinoa and mash to a thick paste.

5. Stir in the soaked linseeds, tomato purée (paste), red (bell) pepper (capsicum), coriander (cilantro), chilli, cumin and remaining salt. Stir in the oats and oat flour until well combined.

6. Divide the mixture into 6 equal pieces and shape them into patties. Place on a non-stick baking tray, cover with clingfilm (plastic wrap) and refrigerate overnight or for at least 4 hours.

7. When ready to start cooking, preheat the oven to 200°C/400°F/gas 6 and cook the tray of patties for 10–12 minutes, until golden brown and crisp. Carefully flip them over and cook for another 10 minutes. (Alternatively, heat a griddle pan until medium hot, then cook the patties in it for 4–6 minutes on each side, or until lightly golden.)

Note: Any left-over burgers can be frozen and eaten another time. Pair with roasted or sautéed vegetables on the side.

DINNER

Quick-fried Greens and Beans

Serves 2

Nutrition per serving: 270 kCal; 14 g protein; 7 g fat; 1 g saturated fat; 28 g carbohydrates; 18 g fibre; 2 g sugars; 380 mg sodium

Preparation: 5 minutes

Cooking: 10 minutes

120 g/4½ oz/4 cups fresh spinach

1 tbsp olive oil

2 garlic cloves, crushed (minced)

1 x 400 g/14 oz can white beans (e.g. cannellini or great northern, from a BPA-free can), drained and rinsed

1 tsp ground cumin

pinch of crushed red pepper flakes

sea salt and freshly ground black pepper

1. Rinse the spinach well and drain in a colander.

2. Heat the oil in a large frying pan (skillet), add the garlic and cook over a medium-high heat for about 30 seconds.

3. Add the spinach, beans, cumin and red pepper flakes, stirring constantly until the spinach wilts and the beans cook through, about 5 minutes. Season with salt and pepper.

Sunshine Soup

Serves 4

Nutrition per serving: 270 kCal; 5 g protein; 11 g fat; 2 g saturated fat; 39 g carbohydrates; 8 g fibre; 16 g sugars; 300 mg sodium

Preparation: 10 minutes

Cooking: 40 minutes

5 carrots

2 sweet potatoes or yams

2 turnips

1 apple

3 tbsp olive oil

2.5 cm (2 in) piece of fresh root ginger, peeled and minced

½ tsp ground turmeric or curry powder

165 g/5½ oz/1 cup cooked chickpeas (garbanzo) or cannellini beans

500 ml/18 fl oz/2 cups water or low-sodium vegetable stock

½ tsp fresh or dried basil, coriander (cilantro) or parsley (optional)

1. Wash carrots, sweet potatoes, turnips and apple and chop into 2.5 cm (1 in) pieces.

2. Heat the oil in a large saucepan over a medium heat and add the chopped ingredients along with some salt and pepper. Add the minced ginger. Cook for 5–10

minutes, then lower the heat and continue cooking until everything has softened, about 30 minutes. Stir in the turmeric or curry powder.

3. Add the chickpeas or beans, then the water or stock and bring to the boil. Reduce heat and cook for another 5–10 minutes on a medium heat, or until the soup is hot.

4. Purée the soup until creamy.

5. Garnish with the herbs and serve.

Quinoa and Broccoli Bowl

Serves 2

Nutrition per serving (not including extra protein option): 340 kCal; 16 g protein; 11 g fat; 52 g carbohydrates; 12 g fibre; 7 g sugars; 400 mg sodium

Preparation: 15 minutes

Cooking: 40 minutes

90 g/3½ oz/½ cup quinoa
150 ml/5 oz/⅔ cup water
1 small head of broccoli, cut into bite-size florets
150 g/5 oz/1 cup cherry tomatoes
3 garlic cloves, chopped
1 tbsp olive oil
2 x 100 g/4 oz wild salmon fillets, skinned (optional)
1 spring onion (scallion), thinly sliced
sea salt and freshly ground black pepper

1. Preheat the oven to 200°C/400°F/gas 6.

2. Rinse the quinoa under cold water and drain well. Place in a saucepan with the water and a pinch of salt and bring to the boil. Reduce the heat and simmer for about 15 minutes, stirring occasionally until all the water has evaporated.

3. Meanwhile, put the broccoli, tomatoes and garlic into a roasting pan, toss with the oil and add salt and pepper to taste. Roast for 10 minutes.

4. Season the salmon (if using) with salt and pepper and nuzzle it into the pan of vegetables. Return to the oven and roast for 12–15 minutes, until the vegetables are tender and the salmon is cooked through. (If you are not including the salmon, skip this step and continue roasting the vegetables for 25 minutes in total, stirring them halfway through.)

5. Add the spring onion (scallion) to the cooked quinoa and fluff with a fork.

6. Divide the quinoa between 2 bowls. Top with the veg mixture and lay the salmon on top.

Latin-inspired Cauliflower 'Rice' and Beans

Serves 4

Nutrition per serving (not including extra protein option): 380 kCal; 15 g protein; 16 g fat; 2 g saturated fat; 48 g carbohydrates; 18 g fibre; 7 g sugars; 800 mg sodium

Preparation: 15 minutes

Cooking: 20 minutes

½ head of cauliflower

1 garlic clove, chopped

1 x 400 g/14 oz can black beans (BPA-free)

4 organic chicken breasts (optional)

2 tomatoes, chopped

½ red onion, chopped

½ jalapeño chilli, chopped

2 tsp ground cumin

1 tsp chilli powder

pinch of cayenne pepper

2 tbsp hot sauce such as Tabasco

2 tbsp chopped chives

1 avocado, flesh diced

sea salt and freshly ground black pepper

1. Cut the cauliflower in half and remove the thick stem. Roughly chop the remainder into florets.

2. Put the cauliflower and garlic into a steamer and steam for 8–10 minutes, until just tender.

3. Drain and rinse the black beans.

4. Season the chicken breasts (if using) with salt and pepper. On a grill or griddle pan at medium-high heat, cook the chicken for about 20 minutes, flipping it over halfway through, until thoroughly cooked.

5. Drain the cauliflower, then pulse briefly in a food processor or blender until it resembles grains of rice.

6. Put the cauliflower into a serving bowl and mix in the beans, tomatoes, onion, chopped chilli, spices and hot sauce.

7. Garnish with the chives and avocado. Finally, top with the chicken, if including.

Substitutions Chart

For those with certain health conditions, allergies or strong food preferences, use the following chart to substitute different foods in recipes.

PRODUCE	ALTERNATIVES
Apple	Berries, grapes, pear, plum
Beetroot (beets)	Golden beet, radish, red cabbage, tomato
Broccoli	Courgettes (zucchini), green cabbage, cauliflower
Carrot	Parsnip, pumpkin, sweet potato, winter squash, yam
Cauliflower	Green or red cabbage, parsnip
Celery	Cucumber, courgettes (zucchini)
Chard (silverbeet)	Greens (collard/spring), green cabbage, kale (Tuscan cabbage), spinach
Cinnamon	Ground ginger, ground turmeric
Coconut water	Diluted fresh juice
Cucumber	Celery, courgettes (zucchini)
Ginger	Turmeric, lemon
Grapefruit	Clementine, orange, tangerine
Grapes	Apple, berries, pear
Kale (Tuscan cabbage)	Greens (collard/spring), spinach, chard (silverbeet), romaine (cos) lettuce

PRODUCE	ALTERNATIVES
Lemon	Lime, orange
Lime	Lemon, orange
Orange	Grapefruit, lemon, lime
Parsley	Rocket (arugula), basil, coriander (cilantro)
Pear	Apple, berries, grapes, plum
Pineapple	Grapefruit, mango, orange
Red cabbage	Broccoli, cauliflower, green cabbage, radish, beetroot (beet)
Romaine (cos) lettuce	Green or red leaf lettuce, radicchio, spinach
Spinach	Greens (collard, spring), kale (Tuscan cabbage), romaine (cos) lettuce, chard (silverbeet)
Sweet green (bell) peppers (capsicums)	Sweet red or yellow (bell) peppers (capsicums), courgettes (zucchini), green beans
Sweet potato	Carrot, parsnip, pumpkin, winter squash, yam
Sweet red (bell) pepper (capsicum)	Sweet yellow or green (bell) pepper (capsicum), tomato
Sweet yellow (bell) pepper (capsicum)	Sweet green or red (bell) pepper (capsicum), yellow squash

Frequently Asked Questions

These are answers to the most common questions asked by those contemplating a Reboot. If your question isn't answered here, visit our website www.rebootwithjoe.com, or Facebook at www.facebook.com/FatSickandNearlyDead.

Q: Will I get enough protein?
A: Many plant foods – broccoli, kale, mushrooms, corn, spinach and collard greens to name just a few – contain a surprisingly high amount of protein. It is highly unlikely that a healthy person would develop a protein deficiency during this 5-Day Reboot. If you choose to Reboot for longer than 15 days, it's best to include a plant-based protein powder, like the Reboot with Joe Protein Powder, in your juices once a day.

Q: What about fibre?
A: It is well established that fibre is an important part of an overall healthy diet, and fruit and vegetables contain lots of it in soluble and insoluble forms. The juicing process extracts the insoluble fibre, leaving you with a liquid that contains just the soluble type. The result is that the health-promoting phytonutrients and enzymes in the soluble fibre are much better absorbed by the body. By removing the fibre

and consuming fruits and vegetables in liquid form, we are providing a nutrient delivery system to our bodies. This offers people who would otherwise have difficulty consuming whole vegetables the opportunity to reap the numerous benefits they have to offer.

Q: Should I exercise during my Reboot?

A: Physical activity is recommended during a Reboot but don't push it. Give yourself a few good days of rest, especially if you don't already regularly exercise. After the first few days, I recommend gentle exercise, such as walking, gentle yoga, t'ai chi, Pilates and swimming. Moving your body during a Reboot has the benefit of working with your plant-powered, nutrient-dense juices to support your immune system, maintain healthy bowel function, promote weight loss, preserve muscle mass while consuming fewer calories, boost your mood and even help to distract you from food cravings.

If you already exercise regularly, you will want to consider decreasing the intensity and duration of exercise during your Reboot, especially in the first few days. You'll want to conserve energy to help your body rest and keep your immune system strong. Since you'll be ingesting fewer calories and macronutrients, such as protein and carbohydrates, than usual, you'll want to downshift your workout accordingly.

Q: How much water should I drink?

A: Even though you will be drinking about 2.4 litres/80 oz of fresh juice daily during the juicing phase of a Reboot, you will need to supplement that intake in order to meet your hydration needs. Aim to drink 1.5–2 litres/48–64 oz in the form of filtered water, herbal teas and coconut water during the day. Most beverages that don't contain caffeine, sugar or alcohol are hydrating: herbal teas, ginger tea with lemon, coconut water, or just plain filtered water are some good examples. If you are constipated, excessively tired, in a hot climate, at a high altitude, engaging in strenuous activity, heavier or taller than average, you might have greater fluid requirements, so should make an extra effort to ensure you are staying hydrated.

Q: How much sleep should I get during my Reboot?
A: Getting adequate sleep is critical to your Reboot because it will assist you with weight loss. Many people feel tired while Rebooting, especially in the first few days, and think they are not getting enough calories or protein, when, in fact, they are just not getting enough sleep. During your Reboot, strive for a minimum of eight hours. Pamper yourself and go to bed early if you're tired. You will probably also find that after the first few days, you will sleep better than you have in years.

Q: Can I use different juice recipes?
A: If you are going to deviate from the Reboot plans by getting creative with your juice recipes (something I encourage), make sure your juice consists mostly of vegetables – about 80 per cent veggies to 20 per cent fruits is a good rule of thumb. While adding a little fruit to the

vegetable juice is a great way to improve its taste and provide very important phytonutrients, if you rely too heavily on fruits, you'll miss out on the wealth of micronutrients locked away in vegetables.

Q: How should I talk to my doctor about Rebooting?
A: Not every doctor is going to be open-minded about a Reboot. Most have been trained to be sceptical about any kind of juicing programme, and tend to think of them as rapid weight-loss schemes that will deprive you of nutrients. A Reboot resets and floods your body with nutrients, and at the same time readjusts your relationship with food, and your doctor certainly understands the importance of fruits and vegetables in your overall health. A Reboot takes your consumption of those to 100 per cent. Fresh juice has highly concentrated amounts of nutrients, enzymes and antioxidants, which are easy to digest and will certainly boost your entire system.

I encourage you to talk openly with your doctor and also to share *Fat, Sick & Nearly Dead* with him or her. Many doctors have been inspired by the movie and now encourage their patients to Reboot, or have even tried it themselves.

Q: Can I use my blender and still get the same results as juicing?
A: No. I recommend using a juicer. Juicing will have a faster effect on weight loss and health improvements in general. There are substantial differences between blending and juicing and you can learn more about them on page 31.

Q: Will I be hungry?
A: If you're hungry, it could be a sign that you are not getting enough nutrients, fluids or calories. Drink more juice and more water. More is better on a Reboot.

Q: I have headaches. What should I do?
A: The headaches that often accompany the first few days of a Reboot can be caused by a number of factors, including caffeine withdrawal. More often than not, drinking more water and juice can help to remedy, or at least reduce, the severity of this common and normal side effect. If after that you still have a headache, drink a glass of coconut water. Still have a headache? Try another juice. Don't forget how helpful walking can be for your headache, as can getting to bed early for some extra sleep.

Q: I ate something – have I failed?
A: I hope by now you realize that eating fruits and vegetables, even if you planned on juicing only, does not constitute failure. It is perfectly OK to eat a salad, baked sweet potato, cooked greens or a piece of fruit when you are Rebooting (it's one of the reasons we have a dinner option!). You might want to juice only, but if you're really hungry or craving something to chew, you will not ruin your Reboot by eating. In fact, it might help you to stick with it.

If you ate something besides a fruit or vegetable, such as a slice of pizza, you're probably not feeling so great physically or emotionally. But you've only failed if you use this as an excuse to quit. Dust yourself off, and get back on the juice wagon. Consider it a setback and that you might now take a little longer to reach your goal, but remember – your Reboot is not ruined.

Q: What if I'm not losing weight?
A: How much juice are you drinking? Remember, you should be drinking three (if you are juicing + dinner) or five (if you are juicing only) 475–600 ml/16–20 oz glasses of juice per day that are predominantly vegetables. Substituting water for juice, or cutting down on the number of juices consumed daily will not help you to lose weight any faster. If you are not losing weight and you have excessive weight to lose, you are probably not consuming enough juice. If you add more juice and still aren't losing weight, try doing more movement and exercise. If that doesn't help, you might want to connect with our community and participate in a Guided Reboot, coached by our nutritionists. If you are not losing weight and have a health condition or take medications, you should speak to your doctor.

Q: Why is caffeine not advised during a Reboot?
A: One of the primary purposes of a Reboot is to give your body a break from many of its daily duties of processing the components contained in the foods and drinks we typically ingest. Caffeine is a substance that is metabolized by the liver. This means that the liver must perform extra work to safely package and remove caffeine's compounds

from our bodies. Ingesting caffeine will therefore give your body additional work to do and could potentially limit the overall effectiveness of the Reboot.

Q: Can I chew gum while juicing?
A: Yes, but look for a natural gum without any artificial sweeteners.

Q: Can I smoke while juicing?
A: Smoking is not advised, since it introduces toxins into the body, which is contrary to the purpose of juicing. The aim is rather to boost your intake of phytonutrients from plants and produce.

Q: Can I Reboot while pregnant or breast-feeding?
A: No. Owing to different nutritional needs during pregnancy and breast-feeding, a Reboot is not advised during those times.

Q: Why does my mouth feel coated?
A: A 'mouth coating' can be an unpleasant side effect of juicing, but it usually goes away after a few days. Try drinking more water and brushing your teeth more often.

Q: Is it OK to use soy milk, rice milk and almond milk in my juice?
A: I don't advise using these products when you are juicing. Although these milks can be healthy choices, best keep them for after your Reboot.

Q: Am I just losing water weight during the juice fast?
A: 'Water weight' includes water that is retained and lost by the body. If you've ever wondered how you can gain or lose a pound in just a few hours, that's likely to be the effect of temporary water weight gain or loss. True weight loss is best measured by tracking your weight over time rather than hour-by-hour or day-by-day. Your weight loss on a Reboot will be a combination of fat, muscle and water, but staying active and drinking enough juice and water will help to preserve muscle mass, promote comparatively more fat loss, and minimize the swings of water weight. For example, my weight loss was 70 per cent fat and 30 per cent muscle. After Rebooting, you can minimize regaining weight by staying active and drinking plenty of water.

Q: Why am I feeling cold on my Reboot and what can I do about it?
A: It's quite common to feel cold on a Reboot, especially during cold weather. This is not necessarily a bad thing, as it sometimes has to do with being in a state of caloric restriction, which can decrease your body temperature. The good news is that it means you are not only in a sweet spot where you can lose weight, but (as research shows) feeling cooler can reduce the signs and processes of aging, protect the body and help reduce your cancer risk. The best 'cure' is to bundle up, sip hot water with lemon and ginger, make broth from your juice pulp, and sip herbal tea. Sometimes a drop in temperature has to do with underlying thyroid

issues. If you have a health condition or take medication, speak with your doctor.

Q: If I lose a lot of weight during and after my Reboot, will I be left with excess skin?

A: While I did not have excess skin, many people who go through extreme weight loss do. It varies and depends on the amount of weight lost, and the distribution of the excess weight. There are surgical and non-surgical options for dealing with excess skin.

Q: Should I take supplements or vitamins?

A: I recommend you stop most non-prescription supplements and vitamins during your Reboot and load up on nutrients from fruits and veggies. However, you may continue to take vitamin D and B12 if you plan on continuing to Reboot. If you have any questions, please ask your doctor.

Q: What if I have food allergies?

A: Your Reboot is naturally free of common allergens, such as dairy, soy, wheat and gluten. If you are allergic, or think you might be, to any fruits or veggies, please do not consume them during your Reboot. See the Substitutions Chart on page 148 for alternative ideas.

Q: What if I take prescription medications?

A: Please continue taking your medications as prescribed, and ask your doctor if you need to make any adjustments. For those of you taking statins to lower cholesterol, please avoid grapefruit and see the Substitutions Chart on page 148 for other ideas. For those taking medication for thyroid conditions, please avoid juicing or eating raw cruciferous vegetables, such as broccoli, cabbage, cauliflower, kale and radish, in large amounts as some of their phytonutrients can interfere with the medication. (It's fine to eat these items cooked.) Check out the Substitutions Chart for additional ideas. Also, please check with your pharmacist or doctor about any drug/food interactions you need to be aware of.

Q: The food on the dinner plan is too much/too little for me. How much should I eat?
A: Eat only as much as feels right to you. Stop when you feel full. Have another juice if you are still hungry. Do what feels right and listen to your body. It knows more than you think!

Q: I don't like coconut water. What can I use instead?
A: Coconut water is a great source of electrolytes, which are important for your Reboot. If you're not fond of the taste, try adding some fresh lemon, lime or orange juice. If you really can't stomach it, we encourage you to drink another juice that is high in electrolytes, such as beetroot, cantaloupe, celery or watermelon.

Q: Can I drink pre-bottled juices? If so, which ones?
A: Freshly made juices are always best, so in the first instance, if you're unable to do the juicing yourself, find a juice bar. Failing that, you can drink bottled juices that are cold-pressed

or HPP (High Pressure Processed) (see page 33). Choose veggie-heavy juices as often as possible.

Q: How long does fresh juice keep?

A: Fresh juice can keep for up to 72 hours as long as it's stored in an airtight container and kept refrigerated. I like to use Kilner jars to store my juices, but any glass or BPA-free plastic container with a lid should work fine. Do not use metal bottles as the juice can react with the metal. Ideally, consume your fresh juice within 24 hours.

Q: Can I freeze my juice?

A: Yes, but it must be frozen immediately after juicing. Frozen juice can keep for 7 to 10 days. If you freeze it in a Kilner jar, leave space at the top for the juice to expand while frozen.

Q: What do I do with the pulp?

A: Have a lot of extra pulp and don't want to waste it? Use it to make some Reboot-friendly vegetable stock (see recipe on page 127). Alternatively, go to www.rebootwithjoe.com for more inspiration. Pulp is also great for garden compost. If you don't have a garden yourself, donate it to someone who does, or take it to a recycling centre that has composting facilities.

Q: Can I use frozen fruit and vegetables?

A: Fresh is preferred, but if you can't find the fruits or vegetables you want to juice in season, you can use frozen (stick with the organic variety). Do remember to defrost the produce before you juice it.

Q: What type of tea should I drink?
A: Herbal, caffeine-free tea is recommended during a Reboot. Aim for organic, all natural if possible.

Q: What is a normal and safe weight loss rate during a Reboot?
A: Everybody loses weight at different rates. That amount will vary, depending on how much weight you have to lose. Those with a lot can lose much more than the average, while those with little to lose might find they drop less.

Q: I feel light-headed and dizzy. What should I do?
A: If you are feeling light-headed, dizzy or weak, you may not be consuming enough calories or electrolytes. Try drinking coconut water or juice when you get dizzy and sip it regularly throughout the day, along with water. If you have concerns, please speak with your doctor.

Q: Is it possible to drink too much juice or eat too many fruits and vegetables?
A: It's really hard to overdo your vegetable and fruit intake, but do remember to listen to your body. If you're hungry, drink more juice. When you're full, take a break and save your juice for later.

Q: I have leg/muscle cramps. What should I do?
A: Leg cramps can be a common symptom of a Reboot. If you get them, increase your electrolyte consumption, along with your intake of dark green leafy vegetables to increase

your levels of magnesium and calcium. Also ensure you are well hydrated.

Q: What should I do if I'm constipated?
A: Difficult, incomplete or infrequent bowel movements are all signs of constipation. In some people, drastic changes to the usual eating pattern can cause the rate of digestion to slow down. If you are having issues with constipation, try drinking more water and increasing the amount you walk.

Q: What if I have diarrhoea?
A: Drink plenty of fluids, but not all consisting of plain water. Diarrhoea can reduce your body's fluid and salt stores, so increase electrolyte-rich fluids, including vegetable stock and unflavoured coconut water.

Q: Why is my pee (or poop) red?
A: You have your first glass of beetroot-based juice and go to the bathroom, and what comes out the other end is red. This phenomenon has a name – beeturia – and it affects about 10–15 per cent of the population. Typically, beeturia is harmless, so keep on juicing.

Q: My poo is green! What's going on?
A: The colour of your waste can naturally range from green to brown, depending on what you eat. As you eat and consume more green vegetables, your stool will naturally turn a greener shade.

Q: My bowel movements have become smaller and less frequent during my Reboot. Is that normal?

A: Yes, this is very common when people extend their Reboots. One way to look at this is that more volume in equals more volume out. Although we are drinking a lot of fluids, we have also removed a lot of the insoluble fibre (pulp) we normally consume, so our stools become smaller and sometimes less frequent.

Q: What are the age requirements for a Reboot?

A: While we believe everyone, no matter what their age, should maximize their consumption of fruit and vegetables, Reboot diet plans are not intended for individuals under the age of 21. If you are under 21 and think a Reboot or a modified Reboot may be right for you, speak to your doctor.

Q: Every time I start juicing I experience symptoms of the common cold. Why is that?

A: Many chronic health complaints, such as headaches, fatigue, diarrhoea, constipation, flatulence, mood swings, aches and pains, sleep disturbances, body odour, oral complaints, flu-like symptoms, skin complaints, reduced immunity, foggy thoughts, asthma, coated tongue and fluid retention can be aggravated initially when you start a juice-only Reboot. But with time and a consistent healthy lifestyle, these flare-ups usually subside and are likely to disappear altogether. Drinking plenty of water, getting enough rest and, ideally, transitioning into your Reboot with healthy plant-based eating (see page 58), can minimize these symptoms. Do bear in mind that not everyone experiences them.

Q: I have nausea/stomach aches/heartburn. What should I do?

A: Sometimes when people start juicing in addition to their normal diet or on a Reboot, they can experience various digestive upsets or changes. To help alleviate these symptoms, make sure you are drinking plenty of water spread throughout the day in small amounts. If there are any individual ingredients that seem to irritate you more than others, eliminate them and adjust the recipe with new or trusted ingredients next time you juice. Removing or reducing the gas-causing vegetables, such as broccoli, cabbage and cauliflower, can also help. Try drinking your juice in smaller portions spread throughout the day, and dilute your juice with 25 per cent water as needed. For nausea, try increasing your intake of hot water with lemon and ginger. Gentle exercise, such as walking, yoga and stretching, has been shown to reduce stomach and digestive upsets.

Q: Is vomiting normal?

A: Vomiting can either be an extreme side effect of stomach discomfort, or you might have caught a stomach bug or virus. You can help alleviate this by sipping organic vegetable broth (not low-sodium), watering down your juices, and consuming more water and electrolytes (e.g. coconut water) throughout the day. You can also try drinking fresh ginger and lemon with hot water to calm your stomach. If vomiting persists or you are concerned, do consult your doctor.

Q: I feel weak and have low energy. What should I do?
A: Increase your electrolyte intake to reduce fatigue, foggy thoughts and headaches. Coconut water is an excellent source of electrolytes.

Q: Why am I bloated and putting on weight?
A: Fluid retention can be another common side effect in the early days of a Reboot. To help alleviate this, make sure you are drinking plenty of fluids throughout the day (which means adequate amounts of juice and coconut water for electrolytes and not too much plain water) and try to get plenty of rest. Walking may help as well. If you take medication, speak to your doctor, as it might need adjusting.

Q: I have a question you don't answer here. What can I do?
A: Go to the community section of www.rebootwithjoe.com where there are many experienced Rebooters who will be happy to offer their help and advice.

Talking to Your Doctor

You might like to download a PDF of juicing facts to share with your doctor to start the conversation. Visit **www.rebootwithjoe.com/for-your-doctor**

Most medical experts agree, and numerous studies are showing, the benefits of consuming fresh fruits and vegetables in the prevention and treatment of obesity, cardiovascular disease, inflammatory conditions and cancer.

It is recommended that anyone with medical problems, on prescription medications or who is interested in participating in the programme for longer than 15 days should consult their doctor before doing so.

Further Information

If you are interested in juicing and Rebooting, please check out www.rebootwithjoe.com. There you can also find out where to watch the movie that started it all, and that movie's sequel. My books are also excellent resources.

Documentary: *Fat, Sick & Nearly Dead* (2010)

Documentary: *Fat, Sick & Nearly Dead 2* (2014)

Joe Cross, *The Reboot with Joe Juice Diet: Lose weight, get healthy and feel amazing* (Hodder & Stoughton, London; Greenleaf Book Group, Austin, TX, 2014)

Joe Cross, *The Reboot with Joe Juice Diet Recipe Book: Over 100 Recipes Inspired by the Film 'Fat, Sick & Nearly Dead'* (Hodder & Stoughton, London; Greenleaf Book Group, Austin, TX, 2014)

Joe Cross, *Reboot with Joe – Fully Charged: 7 Keys to Losing Weight, Staying Healthy and Thriving* (Hodder & Stoughton, London; Greenleaf Book Group, Austin, TX, 2015)

Index

Also available from Joe Cross